Robert C Johansen

The Appraisal
Interview Guide

The Appraisal Interview Guide

Robert G. Johnson

amacom

A Division of American Management Associations

This book was set in Times Roman and Fritz Quadrata by
The Fuller Organization, Inc.
It was designed by Dick Granald, LMD Service for Publishers.
Printer and binder were The Alpine Press.

Library of Congress Cataloging in Publication Data

Johnson, Robert G
   The appraisal interview guide.

   Includes index.
   1. Employees, Ratings of.   2. Performance standards.
3. Work measurement.   I. Title.
HF5549.5.R3J63   658.31'25   79-10704
ISBN 0-8144-5517-4

Third Printing

Contents

Part I
UNDERSTANDING AND PLANNING FOR APPRAISAL INTERVIEWING

Part II
IMPROVING APPRAISAL
INTERVIEWING SKILLS

Part I

UNDERSTANDING AND PLANNING FOR APPRAISAL INTERVIEWING

1

HOW IT ALL BEGAN

The appraisal interview is a private meeting between an employee and his or her immediate supervisor. The subject is the employee's past and present performance. Sometimes the meeting is called a *postappraisal* interview, suggesting that the evaluation has occurred before the two principals meet and that the interview is concerned with communicating the substance of the appraisal.

Appraisal interviews grew out of needs both legitimate and illegitimate.

THE EMPLOYEE'S NEED

The employee has a legitimate need to know how his performance compares with his supervisor's expectations. It is not merely a matter of idle curiosity, but a true need, an essential link of communication between employer and employee. The employer creates a job, establishes (at least in his mind) specifications for it, and hires someone to do it.

The employee seeks evaluation of his performance because he wants his work to be satisfactory to his employer. If it is satisfactory, the employee will feel some sense of security and possibly even pride and a desire to do still better. If his work is not satisfactory, the employee will strive to improve his performance, quit, or resign himself to probable dismissal.

At the same time that the employee seeks evaluation, he may fear it. Unsatisfactory performance may mean being fired, facing embarrassing and irritating criticism, or having to undergo painful behavioral changes. But the employee's need to know how he is doing is more important than the fear of finding out, and most employees are better off knowing than not knowing.

In the absence of specific feedback on performance, some serious problems may develop. The employee may be forming undesirable work habits, but he may assume quite erroneously that the supervisor's silence means approval. ("If the boss didn't like the way I do it, he'd tell me.") At the other extreme, the employee may be doing excellent work but, in the absence of any evaluation by his supervisor, he may not know it. He may abandon good work practices and try others. Wondering what will become of him in an environment that fails to respond to his efforts, he may become disheartened or bitter or look for another job.

Employers must recognize that employees have more than a right to know how they are doing. They have a very strong need to know, and meeting or failing to meet that need will probably have a direct effect on their performance.

It was in part to meet this legitimate need that the appraisal interview was created.

THE EMPLOYER'S NEED

The employee is not the only one with a legitimate stake in the appraisal interview. The employer—specifically, the supervisor—needs to carry out the essential process of communication between employer and employee. If the employee is doing less than satisfactory work and his performance is correctable, the supervisor needs to convey this in the appraisal interview and arrange for improvement. If the employee's work is satisfactory, the supervisor has a stake in that person's future and will use the appraisal interview to promote continued satisfactory performance.

All this suggests that there are minimum intervals at which both employer and employee must review the caliber of work being done and make decisions that will affect future performance. Every employee is an asset to the company, and his contribution needs periodic evaluation.

The appraisal and appraisal interview thus grew out of real needs. The employee needs to know how he or she stands. The employer needs to plan a future course of action regarding the employee's contribution. These needs can be met only through evaluation, and communication about the evaluation.

OTHER NEEDS

Another, less legitimate, reason for appraisals and interviews is to make the personnel system look like a personnel system. A personnel manager who collects and files 6,000 appraisals a year probably appears to have more of a system than someone who collects and files no appraisals. A personnel manager who can proclaim that everyone in his company except the president has a semiannual appraisal interview with his immediate supervisor is a personnel manager with a future. Personnel systems are often judged by volume and activity, and appraisal is one element that usually generates plenty of both.

Several other needs that become intertwined with appraisals, not always to their betterment, should be mentioned. Salary increases have to be determined about once a year, and this function is sometimes attached to the appraisal process as an uneasy rider. The appraisal form is a convenient place for discussing certain aspects of employees' performance that some supervisors never talk about otherwise. Then, too, appraisals and interviews are sometimes executed because "it's policy," although the original intention may have long been lost.

The result of all of these needs, real and imagined, relevant and irrelevant, is an organization policy or practice that requires supervisors to appraise the performance of subordinates at stated intervals and to talk about the appraisal with each subordinate. The interval is usually six months or one year, an appraisal form is usually supplied, and enforcement varies from rigid to zero.

IS THERE NO OTHER WAY?

The practical mind wonders whether a supervisor truly needs all this apparatus to tell a subordinate how good his or her work is. The answer is a resounding yes and no.

No, it is not necessary because evaluation is not such a tremendous feat. It can easily be accomplished by supervisors of reasonable competence without all the forms and policies and training that personnel appraisal seems to entail. Yes, it is necessary because it has been demonstrated in many organizations that employees get little or no feedback on their performance unless supervisors are required to give it. Just why this is so we will consider later.

In many types of jobs, bosses and subordinates work in such proximity and with such candor that they never have any question about the job being done. With supervisors and employees who have built up strong mutual trust and respect, an appraisal interview as such is wholly superfluous. One can indeed make a case that communicating performance evaluation is one of the essential day-to-day tasks of supervisors and that semiannual or annual performance evaluations are evidence that supervisors are suspected of not doing their jobs.

The case for continuous performance evaluation is a convincing one. In the ideal organization, with all supervisors performing optimally, the question of periodic formal performance appraisal would never arise. Every employee would know precisely how he or she is doing at all times. Poor performers would be helped to become competent. Good performers would be kept at a high level and groomed for greater responsibilities.

Considering that the science of management is so young, these ideals are not beyond attainment. But what we have learned so far is that most supervisors fail to keep subordinates informed of the quality of their work. The appraisal and the interview are dictated by policy to ensure, within the limits of competence and enforcement, that employees will not be kept in the dark indefinitely. To those who complain that this is a poor substitute for a steady supply of feedback, we can only sigh, "Amen."

2

COMMON PROBLEMS IN PERSONNEL APPRAISAL

Many personnel systems require periodic appraisal of employees because managers, supervisors, and foremen often give inadequate feedback to employees on their job performance. That very fact tells us something about the probable success of attempts to give feedback in conformity with the system.

Suppose a supervisor, for whatever reason, fails to give his subordinates regular and complete feedback on their performance. His organization installs a personnel system, part of which calls for him to do what he has historically failed to do—sit down with employees and talk about their performance. What are his chances of success?

If the organization's "system" begins and ends with a policy to compel such a confrontation, the chances of success are poor. If there are many supervisors like this one in the organization, the whole process is threatened. But materials such as this book are testimony to the belief that people can *learn* to give regular and complete feedback, to the betterment of the organization and the individual.

Part of learning to do it right is knowing some of the likely pitfalls. What are some of the ways that personnel appraisal and appraisal interviewing can go off the track?

AVOIDANCE

The most obvious and possibly most common way to botch appraisal of a subordinate, or a conference with him about that appraisal, is to avoid doing it at all. This may take several forms. The supervisor may simply ignore the appraisal form and the policy requiring its use. He may complete the appraisal form and return it to the personnel office without ever discussing it with the subordinate. Or he may ask the subordinate to complete an appraisal of himself, sign it, and send it in, again without discussion.

One of the more subtle ways of avoiding real appraisal is to complete the form in positive fashion, show the employee how positive it is, and send it in without ever digging beneath the surface. All the requirements are thus met without the supervisor's ever facing the issue of appraisal or talking openly about the appraisal with the subordinate.

Avoidance occurs for a variety of reasons. Some supervisors are embarrassed and afraid to talk freely with subordinates about their performance. Some honestly feel they have a constant exchange of such information with subordinates and have no need for such an encounter. Some supervisors are buried so deeply in nonsupervisory duties that appraisal, along with many other important functions, just fails to get scheduled. Then there are supervisors who, for various reasons, find the process abhorrent, worthless, or even detrimental and avoid it if they can.

ARGUMENT

One of the risks in appraisal interviewing is disagreement. If the supervisor sits in judgment, the employee will feel obligated to rise to his own defense. Part of his defense may consist of counterattack, against which the supervisor will then defend. In no time at all, what began as a reasoned discussion of one person's performance becomes an ugly, vindictive argument. What turns appraisals and appraisal interviews into arguments?

An accumulation of hostility, mutual or otherwise, can lead to an argumentative interview. A supervisor and subordinate who have few opportunities to speak honestly may build up reservoirs of hostility. The appraisal interview, as one of the few opportunities for candor, becomes the valve that releases the pent-up negative feelings. The remedy is, of course, to find ways to keep the channels open between interviews on a daily basis. An environment of candor and respect not only defuses the appraisal interview's potential explosiveness but also reduces the need for the interview itself.

Lack of interviewing skill on the part of supervisors is a common cause of argument in an appraisal interview. If supervisors do not know the objective of the interview, they may be heavily judgmental, encounter defensiveness, and find themselves in an argument they have to win. A little knowledge and a few simple skills can prevent such an argument.

UNEXPRESSED HOSTILITY

Sometimes the employee becomes hostile during an appraisal interview but does not express his negative feelings. The boss leaves the interview feeling, "That went a lot better than I thought it would; he took it like a lamb." The employee leaves feeling, "That miserable so-and-so thinks he's got me just where he wants me; I'll show him."

In this situation the two people are unable to communicate, in part because the supervisor lacks interviewing skills. The supervisor irritates, but the employee is afraid to show his irritation or perhaps even to express his opinion. The boss may do all the talking and never give the employee a chance. He dominates the interview and comes away thinking he has "won" it. Actually, he has done more damage by holding the interview than he would have by avoiding it.

LOST IN THE FORM

The appraisal form itself is at the bottom of many appraisal interviews that accomplish very little. The form itself may be an exhaustive tome attempting to deal with too much, or it may be misused by the appraiser.

The variety of appraisal forms offered by organizations is testimony to the total absence of agreement among personnel specialists as to what appraisals are for. Some forms are so open-ended and lacking in substance, with so much left to the user's imagination, that almost anything can happen. Others cover 100 items—including the shine on the employee's shoes and the smile on his face. This type of form spreads the reader's attention over so many different matters that both supervisor and subordinate become bogged down in a welter of detail.

One national sales organization requires six to eight detailed field reports on each salesman per year, plus even more detailed semiannual evaluations and annual forced-choice rankings. These reports involve nearly 600 data items per salesman per year—all to be recorded, discussed, submitted, filed, and presumably referred to by someone at the home office from time to time. About 100,000 data items are collected for the sales force in one year.

As we will see in later chapters, effective appraisal interviews depend in part on the establishment of limited, attainable objectives. Appraisal forms requiring dozens or hundreds of items of information do not lend themselves to the pursuit of limited objectives.

THE HIDDEN PRESENCE

Many organizations require that copies of the periodic performance appraisal be sent to other offices for filing and reference. This practice is much like bugging the room where the interview is held, with the knowledge of both participants. They both know that the appraisal is being monitored by one or more higher authorities, and both play the game required by that knowledge.

The employee feels, probably with some justification, that the appraisal form will be consulted by people who have some say in his future. His chief interest is thus to obtain a maximum of favorable grades and a minimum of unfavorable ones. Quite naturally, he wants to look as good as possible. He cares what his immediate supervisor thinks of him, but more important he is concerned with what those up the line think of him. What if his name comes up for promotion? What if this sheet of paper is consulted?

The supervisor has his own problems with the appraisal form. After all, he is being monitored too. What if his judgments appear too harsh or too lax? What if he gives too many 2s and not enough 4s? What if his judgments of the employee are counter to those of the manager up the line?

The hidden presence of other parties, dictated by the practice of sending appraisals to other offices, puts pressure on employee and supervisor alike. It leads them not to do a thorough or an accurate or a constructive job, but above all to try to come out looking good. The attempts of both parties to succeed in this game may completely overshadow any gains to be obtained by appraisal and conversation.

MISTAKEN IMPRESSIONS

Even a well-conducted, constructive appraisal and interview can produce problems. Often the subordinate comes away with the distinct impression that his work is highly satisfactory *and that as a result he may expect a promotion.* The supervisor may never have said this at all (although the mistake of saying it has been made too). But by his failure to limit the meaning of the appraisal for the employee, and to make clear that even his unqualified endorsement guarantees nothing, he leads tHe employee to expect a promotion. When, for reasons quite apart from the employee's performance, no promotion is forthcoming, disappointment, frustration, and even hostility toward the supervisor may result.

COMBINATIONS

We have noted earlier the annual need to make salary adjustments. This review is sometimes mistakenly coupled with the appraisal interview, with disastrous results. To see why this is so, put yourself in the role of the employee.

Your supervisor calls you in and together you discuss your recent performance. Somewhere during the interview he notes that he is recommending a $400 pay raise for you. Consider now the total impact of that meeting: What will weigh more—what he said about your performance or the $400?

For most people, the message of such an interview

is dollars. And if there is some discrepancy between what the boss says about their performance and what he plans to pay for it—as there usually is—the result is far from constructive. The fact is that most supervisors have little to say about subordinates' pay and very often are in the position of merely suggesting ways to divide up a "pot" available for increases. In no way can most supervisors match up pay and performance, and the lesson to be learned is that performance appraisal and salary review are not compatible.

TRIVIA

Some supervisors so misunderstand the function of periodic appraisal that they squander it by reciting an assortment of minor infractions and annoyances perpetrated by the employee. This has at least two unfortunate effects: It wastes the appraisal on trivia, and it leaves minor day-to-day matters untouched except at annual or semiannual interviews.

No attempt has been made here to catalog all the ways in which appraisals and appraisal interviews can become derailed. Enough of the common ones have been noted to demonstrate that personnel managers and supervisors at all levels have a bear by the tail when they take on personnel appraisal. Beginning with the next chapter, we will address the subject of taming that bear.

3

THE MODEL
APPRAISAL INTERVIEW

One might suppose, especially in light of the previous chapter, that an appraisal interview is so fraught with pitfalls that it should be avoided at any cost. Not so. The appraisal interview is a useful personnel tool, and the supervisor need not be a psychologist or any other kind of specialist to conduct one effectively.

In this chapter we will examine a model for an effective appraisal interview, using later chapters to develop some of the elements. The model has five essential characteristics:

1. The interview is one step in a continuing process.
2. The interview has limited objectives.
3. The interview is controlled by the supervisor, not by a form.
4. The supervisor employs a strategy relevant to the objectives.
5. The supervisor uses learned skills.

APPRAISAL AS A CONTINUING PROCESS

The appraisal interview is neither the beginning nor the end of anything. It is a middle step in a cycle that begins when an employee is hired to do a specific job and ends when he leaves it. If the other steps have been omitted or short-circuited, there is little hope for the appraisal interview.

The first step in the continuing process is to define the job—a principle that appears in most personnel manuals. The trouble is that job descriptions seldom go beyond formal job specifications. The very language of such documents all but obscures what is expected of the incumbent: "Shall give leadership to programs of emphasis developed by management," "Responsible for the execution of company sales policies," "Shall direct the activities of subordinate staff members." Confronted with the language of most job descriptions, the new employee can only throw up his hands and ask, "Yes, but what do you *really* want me to do?" (But that is not what the employee says. He or she is more likely to respond with "I see.")

One manager wanted more than anything else for his staff members to keep people off his back. He hated confrontations, was afraid of people, and didn't like controversy. Any subordinates who could successfully isolate him from having to deal with people and issues met his expectations. Naturally, he never conveyed his performance objectives for subordinates in words. People had to work for him long enough to discover them for themselves.

The first step in the continuing process of managing subordinates is to define the job. The second is to communicate the job definition clearly to employees. It is not just handing them written job specifications. It means leveling with them as to what you really expect. Most supervisors at this point labor under a severe handicap. Either they do not have enough insight to know what they really expect of a subordinate or they know perfectly well but lack the honesty to convey it. The manager described above who wanted people kept off his back lacked both.

It is at this very point in the cycle that the appraisal and interview may be doomed. If the supervisor is unable or unwilling to convey what he really wants of the employee, he leaves to chance that the employee will discover it. And only if the employee discovers what is expected does he have any hope of delivering.

The cycle is off to a good start if the employee knows or correctly guesses what is required of him. Over time, most employees will try to deliver what they perceive is expected. Then comes the next step in the cycle: appraisal.

In later chapters we will discuss the mechanics of appraisal. Here we will limit ourselves to understanding where appraisal comes in the sequence. The job is defined and the expectations are conveyed to the employee, who works at his job for a time. Then an evaluation is necessary—a comparison of performance with expectations. This may be done before or during the associated step called the appraisal interview.

Evaluation leads to discussion. If productive, discussion leads to plans for improvement in performance. (There are exceptions that will be discussed later.) Performance goes on for a time, appraisal occurs again, and the cycle repeats. This is shown schematically in Figure 1.

Figure 1. *The appraisal cycle.*

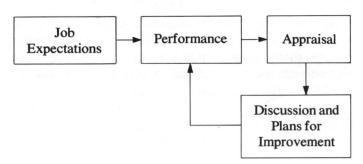

Note that it is the *process* that is cyclical and repetitive, not the *content*. With any kind of luck, the supervisor will not, for example, see the need for better work habits, make plans to improve them, and carry out an endless cycle of needing better work habits and not getting them. The appraisal interview should be viewed as the natural outgrowth of defining a job and putting someone to work doing it. The process is not unlike tuning up an engine at regular intervals. It is a review of effectiveness and efficiency, and its objective is to maintain or develop performance according to standards.

LIMITED OBJECTIVES

The appraisal interview should have limited but useful objectives. Most appraisal interviews are held to meet the personnel system's demand that one be conducted. This is a limited objective but not a constructive one. The supervisor, commonly faced with an appraisal form calling for a great many judgments, often feels that the purpose of the interview is to convey all the judgments. But we must ask why.

The interview itself is not a very useful occasion. Objectives for the interview must be expressed in terms of what is to happen afterward. Thus we can never with any certainty judge an appraisal interview immediately afterward as successful or good or useful. We must wait and see what happens.

Appraisal forms often suggest a great many areas for evaluation. Few of us would score consistently high on them. If an appraisal form were made extensive enough, we would all fail. And if that were true, it would not be a reasonable objective to try to gain improvement in a dozen or more areas of subperfection. We must limit ourselves to the possible. In later chapters we will consider such limited objectives in greater detail.

CONTROL BY THE SUPERVISOR

The model appraisal interview is controlled by the supervisor. Its content is not controlled by an appraisal form or by the fact that the form must be sent on to another authority. This sounds like a big order, but it is a lot simpler than it might appear. The next chapter details how it can be done.

We have already noted that appraisal forms tend to be either too general or too voluminously specific. As a result, they do not make good guides for appraisal interviews and should not be used as such. We have also noted that when an appraisal form must be submitted to an additional authority, this fact can dominate a meeting. This obstacle too can be dealt with.

The supervisor who conducts the appraisal must have absolute control over it. He sets its objectives. He determines what will be talked about. He keeps the interview on the track.

A STRATEGY RELEVANT TO OBJECTIVES

The way a supervisor goes about planning and conducting an appraisal interview depends on what he or she hopes to accomplish. It should be obvious that an appraisal interview with a 59-year-old veteran employee is not the same thing as one with a 26-year-old hot shot. An employee whose performance is satisfactory needs a different kind of interview from that needed by one whose performance is unacceptable.

In later chapters we will take up in detail the strategies needed to meet various interview objectives. At this point we should note that each situation suggests objectives; objectives suggest strategies.

INTERVIEWING SKILL

Although an effective appraisal interview requires skill on the part of the appraiser, skill alone will not do the job. There are too many other elements, as shown in this chapter. But none of the other elements will get the job done right in the absence of the appraiser's skill.

In a good appraisal interview the employee does most of the talking. In order to ensure this, the supervisor must know something about asking questions. Are there different forms of questions, or are all questions alike? Can questions do any more than elicit information?

How can the supervisor avoid getting the subordinate's dander up? Or his own? Can he foresee and prevent arguments, or defuse them if they start?

How can the supervisor keep the interview on the subject? How can he improve the likelihood that something beneficial will come out of the interview? How can he get an employee to want to improve his performance?

The answers to all these questions are discussed in later chapters on specific skills. A supervisor can do all these difficult things after he learns how.

Are you about to undertake an appraisal interview? Then answer these questions before you proceed:

1. Does the employee whose performance is to be appraised know already—really—what is expected of him?
2. Have you developed one or more specific objectives for the interview in terms of desired outcomes?
3. Will you control the interview and not let the appraisal form do it?
4. Have you developed a strategy for the interview?
5. Do you have the necessary skill to do what you want to do?

If the answer to any of these questions is no, you are not ready to schedule the interview.

4

THE TYRANNY OF THE APPRAISAL FORM

The appraisal form, intended to be a useful personnel tool, often ensures that nothing really productive comes out of the appraisal process. This may be true because of defects in the form itself, problems in how the form is used, or misuse of the form by the appraiser. Yet there are ways to get around a bad form, conform with organization policy, and have constructive appraisals.

DESIGN OF THE FORM

It would be pointless to catalog all the errors in appraisal form design. A few examples will illustrate the kinds of problems in many forms.

We have already noted one common defect in appraisal forms: they cover too much. In developing a comprehensive form, some personnel specialists seem to overlook the fundamental question of how appraiser and appraisee will react to all these judgments. They fail to consider the unlikelihood that so vast a catalog of deficiencies will be parlayed into improved employee performance. In fact, the more we examine such personnel tools, the more we must wonder why so many appraisal form designers seem to know so little about people.

More than a few appraisal form designers are unable to resist inserting a catalog of personal characteristics into their forms. So we find supervisors attempting to measure qualities like "attitude," "initiative," and "tact" in the course of appraising subordinates. How is Jones's attitude on a scale of 1 to 5?

Buried in such impossible measurements is, of course, the truth that Jones's attitude is indeed a matter of possible concern for his supervisor. The problem lies not in introducing "attitude" or "initiative" or "tact" into the appraisal process, but in attempting to elicit objective measurements of these higher-order abstractions.

We do not know what the form designer had in mind when he put in "attitude" as a characteristic to be evaluated. Nor do we know what Jones's supervisor meant when he gave Jones a 3 in attitude. Nor does Jones's plant manager know what the supervisor meant; he has his own ideas about attitude. Yet we all treat Jones's appraisal form as if a 3 in attitude were just as objective and meaningful as "4 days lost because of sickness."

"Attitude," in fact, is one of the more offensive higher-order abstractions appearing on appraisal forms. Salesman Brown may consistently exceed quota, act with scrupulous honesty, and break his neck for his customers. But along the line Brown may incur a written reputation for having a "bad attitude," whatever that is. It may mean that he is a Democrat among Republicans, a straight among philanderers, a teetotaler among drunks, or just someone somebody doesn't happen to like. The point is that appraisers have the power to create an apparently objective and possibly indelible record that shows an employee with a good performance record having poor judgment or a bad attitude or a lack of aggressiveness.

At this point we must review the whole question of why we appraise performance in the first place. Is it to create a record of judgments that can be used indefinitely for or against an employee? Or is it to lend a hand to the faltering, encourage the productive, and retain the excellent? Having decided which objective we want, we can adapt our appraisal tools to meet it.

Another common weakness of appraisal forms is that they use ranges of point values, suggesting a continuum that does not in fact exist. They list characteristics or criteria and require a numerical rating on each. (See, for example, Figure 2.) The range seems to

Figure 2. *Rating scale.*

	1	2	3	4	5
Completes reports on time					
Understands his job					
Accepts criticism					

provide a lot of latitude, but directions supplied with the form often narrow it quickly. We are told, for example, that we must be parsimonious with 5s so they will "have meaning," and that 1s and 2s are grievous and must be corrected immediately. Given that information, we are effectively confined to 3s and 4s or, if we were to substitute adjectives for numbers, "satisfactory" and "unsatisfactory."

There is a problem with numbers even if the range is as wide as it looks. The appraiser may read an entirely different value into a number than a subsequent reviewer of the appraisal will. The appraiser, for example, may check "4—needs improvement," meaning that in this respect the employee is just a little under standard. The later reviewer may read this 4 as an irredeemable deficiency.

Another common weakness of appraisal forms is the

casual use of adjectives. A notable example is the mixed batch of adjectives among which the appraiser is expected to select. Such a list might typically contain these words: ambitious, sincere, shrewd, tactful, exploitative, candid, devious, calculating, taciturn.

Supervisors are also called on by some organizations to make periodic forced-choice rankings of subordinates, in connection with or apart from routine appraisals. In effect, this is a subjective ranking of subordinates from best to worst:

> Smith
> Jones
> Brown
> Miller
> Davis

There is probably some value in having the supervisor do such a ranking for his own purposes. Surely he needs to know his best performers so he can help develop them for promotion. Surely he needs to know his poorest so that they can be brought to a higher standard of performance or discharged. But such a ranking cannot disclose, for example:

☐ That this supervisor's standards for ranking are not the same as those of his peers.

☐ That top man Smith might be at the bottom in another group.

☐ That bottom man Davis just joined the group yesterday.

☐ That fourth-rated Miller is the boss's son-in-law and would have been fired long ago on the basis of performance alone.

☐ That third-rated Brown would show up at the top if the records were kept objectively.

Shall we go on? The forced-choice ranking cannot be interpreted by any party other than the person doing the ranking. But it is found in appraisal systems

—not, to be sure, on employees' appraisal forms but among the personnel chores of many supervisors.

Appraisal forms and devices, including well-intentioned ones, often corrupt the appraisal process, either reducing appraisal to a meaningless neutrality or actually having a negative effect on performance.

MISUSE OF THE FORM

Even good appraisal forms can be deadly in the hands of unknowing supervisors. Let's look at some examples.

To use the form as the basis of the appraisal interview is almost certainly to undermine the purpose of the interview. Under such conditions, the supervisor cannot escape the role of judge, and in that role his ability to obtain improved performance is greatly impaired. Whatever else he says or does, the form serves as irrefutable evidence that the principal function of appraisal is to create a record of judgments.

Some supervisors fall into even more grievous traps with appraisal forms. For example, they may fill out the forms and send them back without consulting the employee. This meets the need of the system for paper flow but communicates nothing whatever to the employee about his performance. And we must wonder what kind of relationship exists between supervisor and employee when the supervisor does this as a matter of course.

Perhaps the worst abuse of appraisal forms occurs when the supervisor changes parts of the appraisal *after* discussing it with the employee. It is usually a foregone conclusion that the last-minute changes in evaluation will be down rather than up. Such a practice is bold dishonesty and should, when discovered, result in removal of the supervisor. The practice of having the employee sign and retain a copy of the appraisal was developed to counteract this common deceit.

IMPROVEMENT BY THE ORGANIZATION

This section suggests some principles that an organization can use to attack the tyranny of the appraisal form. Suggestions for individuals in an unenlightened system follow in the next chapter.

Principle 1: Appraisal and discussion of appraisal details are personal and privileged. Copies of written appraisals should never be placed in the hands of anyone except the two principals.

Principle 2: Most supervisors need a form and other materials in order to carry out effective appraisals. Organizations should develop and provide materials for this purpose, recognizing that forms will often be adapted to situations and that none will be returned for central filing after appraisal.

Principle 3: Appraisal forms should call for (1) some objective data on the employee's performance during the period covered by the appraisal (number and extent of absences from work, number of units produced, projects completed, units sold, and so forth) and (2) aspects of job performance to be rated either satisfactory or unsatisfactory, with space for comment on each. (See Figure 3.)

Figure 3. *Objective data on a salesman's job performance.*

	Sat.	Unsat.	Comment
Use of sales bag			
Use of samples			
Presentation effectiveness			

Principle 4: A new supervisor should supervise his people for a period of time and complete appraisals

with them at least once before referring to appraisals made by the previous supervisor. This avoids what may be called the Pygmalion syndrome (See Chapter 17).

Principle 5: The most effective way to develop an appraisal record is to have the supervisor and the subordinate work out the appraisal together. However, the creation of a record is only incidental to the appraisal process and should not be seen as the primary purpose.

Principle 6: In order to ensure that personnel officers and higher line authorities know that the appraisal process is working and are given information on the status of each employee, a supervisor's report akin to the example shown in Figure 4 should be required at the intervals prescribed for appraisal.

Principle 7: To purge itself of the tyranny of the appraisal form an organization should destroy the accumulated appraisals, forced-choice rankings, and other articles in its files. This act of corporate amnesty will have a positive effect, even if there is no follow-up.

Figure 4. *Sample report by district manager on completion of a semiannual appraisal.*

TO: Regional Manager

On this date I have worked with the subject to complete and discuss a semiannual appraisal. Our evaluation is summarized by this report, as is the follow-up action dictated by the classification.

CLASSIFICATION	FOLLOW-UP ACTION
__Performance in general is adequate for current position.	Analyze consequences of possible promotion and plan replacements as needed.

(Continued)

Subject is believed
promotable to:
__Larger territory
__Sales trainer
__Assistant district
   manager
__HQ staff position:

_____

__Performance in general
is adequate for current
position.
Subject is believed
potentially promotable
after further experience
and development.
Tentative calendar
objective for
promotability: _____

1. Work with subject to
   prepare development
   plans.

2. Implement the plans.

__Performance in general
is adequate for current
position.
Subject is not to be
developed for promotion
because of:
__Personal reasons
__Perceived lack of
   potential

1. Discuss with subject
   means of maintaining
   performance at current
   level or greater on
   present job.

2. Discuss with subject the
   limitations on future
   promotability.

__Performance in general
is not adequate for
current position.
Subject is being
developed to achieve
adequate performance
levels. Tentative calendar
objective for this
achievement: _____

1. Discuss with subject the
   areas of greatest
   concentration and make
   specific plans for
   improvement.

2. Provide opportunity for
   feedback and further
   progress review.

_____   _____   _____

Salesman   Manager   Date

5

LIVING WITH THE APPRAISAL FORM (OR GETTING ALONG WITHOUT IT)

More than a few readers of this book will be part of an organization that does not heed the principles outlined in the previous chapter. This chapter is addressed to individuals who conscientiously want to conduct a productive appraisal but whose company makes this difficult, either by inappropriate use of an appraisal form or by not having a form.

WHEN COPIES OF THE FORM ARE REQUIRED

If your organization requires that one or more copies of a completed appraisal form be submitted to personnel officers or someone up the hierarchy, you must work within that policy. There are four basic ways to work with an appraisal form, and most organizations do not require compliance with any one way.

1. The supervisor completes the appraisal form and then discusses its contents with the subordinate. This practice is undesirable because it requires the

supervisor to play the role of judge, a role that is incompatible with the appropriate role of *facilitator.*

2. The subordinate completes the appraisal form on himself and then discusses his self-appraisal with his supervisor. This is a somewhat better practice, but it still casts the supervisor in the undesirable role of judge—in this case, judging the judgments of his subordinate.

3. The subordinate and the supervisor each complete a copy of the appraisal form and then bring them together and resolve differences. This is a still better method, but it lends itself to disagreement and argument, since both parties will feel obligated to defend what they have written.

4. The supervisor and the subordinate review a blank appraisal form independently, making no marks on it, and then come together and complete an appraisal of the subordinate. This method is the best of all, since it has the advantage of joint discussion and consideration without the liability of any written preconceptions.

I recommend that the fourth approach to appraisal be used. It should be introduced to the employee in the spirit, if not the words, of the following:

"Here is a copy of the company appraisal form. Management requires that one be completed yearly and a copy sent to personnel. Have a good look at the form, and I will too. Let's meet Wednesday morning to fill one out together. Then later on we can get together and concentrate on the really important things about your job performance and your future, and we won't have to create any records at that time."

When you and your subordinate meet, make it clear again that you are complying with company policy. Take the items on the form one at a time. Ask the employee what he thinks before offering your own opinion of his rating on each item. Employees tend to understate their ratings, and you will be in a position to suggest that several items be rated higher than the employee proposes. This will compensate for those few items on which you feel the rating should be below what the employee suggests. At all times make certain the employee knows that you are only creating a record, not trying to get at the heart of the matter. The session will be successful if the record you create is acceptable to you, to the employee, and to the organization.

Discussion with your subordinate as you complete the appraisal form may suggest some topics to be covered in the "real" appraisal interview. If so, make note of this for consideration during the interview.

The objective of the procedure suggested here is twofold: (1) to comply with the organization's requirement for a completed appraisal form and (2) to be free to conduct a purposeful appraisal interview without the constrictions of a form. Once you've completed the form and sent it in, you can follow the suggestions below, just as if there were no form.

WHEN NO FORM IS REQUIRED

If your organization does not require that copies of appraisal forms be submitted, or if it does and that formality has been carried out, the appraisal process can proceed unencumbered. The steps are as follows:

1. Define the job expectations.
2. Appraise the performance of the employee.
3. Plan the appraisal interview.
4. Conduct the interview.

We will take up these steps in subsequent chapters.

6

DEFINING JOB EXPECTATIONS

As we have seen, formal job descriptions differ from true job expectations. Why is this so? The question is worth extensive research in itself, and we can only investigate a few of the answers here.

One reason is that many formal job descriptions are written centrally and made to apply to many positions. A personnel officer and a national sales manager, for example, may collaborate on a job description for all the company's salesmen. In so doing, they may create an effective set of criteria for appraising 100 salesmen's performance. But they also will eliminate those individualized job expectations that originate with the salesmen's first-line managers.

Another reason for the difference between formal job descriptions and actual expectations is the language of the job description itself. Job descriptions are often written in legalistic and nonbehavioral terms. "Shall be responsible for maintaining effective relations with the company's clients" is typical language. It places a mighty burden on the shoulders of the incumbent but gives no hint of what he must do to carry this weight. In truth, job descriptions are often beyond understanding because they are at too high a level of abstraction.

Still another explanation for the difference between written job descriptions and actual job expectations is simply that most of us would not dare to place on file the real expectations we have for some jobs. They would be too homely, too blunt, too—well, truthful. "Keep people off my back" might be one. Or "Stay out of trouble." "Put in your time." "Meet quota."

THE CHOICE FOR APPRAISAL

A supervisor who sets out to appraise the performance of a subordinate often has a choice before him. He can appraise in terms of a preexisting job description or he can appraise in terms of his personal expectations for that job. There is probably a huge difference between the two, and chances are only one set of criteria is written down.

The easy choice is to appraise in terms of the formal job description. This is seldom the more fruitful course. The written job description, more often than not, simply does not cover the real issues. When the appraisal is finished, the employee still will not know how well he measures up to what is expected of him. The whole process—appraisal, discussion, and planning—will have the unreal air of a role play, an academic exercise. The harder course for the supervisor is to try to sort out what he really expects of *this person* in *this job* at *this time*. It may be all the harder if he discovers that he does not really know.

A common copout is to ask the employee to define his job. Most good personnel manuals advise against this, for the good reason that employees tend to define their jobs in terms of what they already do or would like to do rather than in terms of the organization's needs. This is not to suggest that employees should have no voice in writing their job descriptions, because they often can help to define their jobs in constructive ways. The error lies, not in asking employees to help define their jobs, but in shifting the total burden to them.

LISTING JOB EXPECTATIONS

The immediate supervisor, if he is competent, knows the organization's short-term and long-term needs in his area. He knows the work that has to be done. He knows what it takes in terms of knowledge, skills, and manpower. It is with this kind of knowledge that he begins to define an individual employee's job.

Using whatever formal job description is available, the supervisor can begin to jot down a few areas that he recognizes to be of most importance *to him*. It is not "the company" the subordinate must please; it is the boss. The boss determines how he wants the job done, conveys this to the employee, and then measures performance in those terms.

A sales manager might jot down these criteria for a particular salesman: "Meet quota," "Turn in reports on time," "Keep customers happy." On further thought, he comes to see that "Turn in reports on time" is especially important to him. If the salesman's reports are late, the manager's reports are late, and then the manager gets flak from *his* manager. And since the top manager may see timely reports as the highest of all priorities, this matter becomes—whether anyone down below likes it or not—a high priority in personnel appraisal.

Likewise, as the sales manager reflects on the performance of the individual salesman, he finds he cannot put out of his mind the fact that the salesman has bad breath! Now what can he do about that? If the salesman's job requires frequent face-to-face meetings with customers, and if offensive breath could interfere with the sales function, it is certainly reasonable to make the breath problem a subject for discussion. (If the salesman did his selling only by telephone, the matter might be overlooked.)

Many an employee performs satisfactorily and indeed splendidly in every respect but one. Sometimes that one respect is the single obstacle to his achieving all that both he and his company want. If there is any hope of correction, the matter must be raised in the appraisal interview.

Another example: A small businessman, anticipating future expansion, hires an employee he expects to become a supervisor of others within three years. At the end of an appraisal period, the employer must find out just how far the employee has progressed toward that goal and what remains to be done. In this case the appraisal is not limited to performance on the present job but also includes development toward a higher job. If the employer believes, for example, that the employee's experience in cost estimating is inadequate for future supervision, that deficiency must be addressed at appraisal time.

The process by which a supervisor can get hold of the real job expectations for a particular person and job thus begins with questions like these:

- □ "What do I really expect this person to do on the job?"
- □ "What are his major strengths and weaknesses in doing these things?"
- □ "What personal characteristics or habits block greater achievement?"
- □ "What's ahead for this person? Why?"

Some readers will recognize that, unless the supervisor is careful with such questions, he will wind up generating a new appraisal form for each employee. This is a valid concern. The way out of the trap is to concentrate on matters of major importance and avoid trivia. The objective is not to develop a whole catalog of minutiae, but to bring out for examination the most important elements in job performance and potential.

The resulting notes will not resemble a formal job description or an appraisal form. Rather, they will simply list, in the supervisor's own handwriting, his subjective view of the employee's job expectations so that he can undertake the appraisal. Some examples follow.

SECRETARY:	Being on hand, not late or absent or elsewhere
	Accuracy in typing
	Filing
	Screening calls
SHOP FOREMAN:	Scheduling work
	Keeping workers happy
	Productivity
	Handling problems without bothering the supervisor
DISTRICT SALES MANAGER:	Reports complete and on time
	Salesman turnover
	Quota
	Recruiting
	Lost accounts

These examples are not meant to be comprehensive or to represent models for employees with similar job titles. They merely represent what one supervisor decided were the principal job expectations of one particular person at one time. Another supervisor might not have any such expectations of similar employees.

To get an idea of his own priorities, the supervisor seeking to appraise can rank-order the items on his list. His greatest problem in doing this will be trying to be honest in deciding what he values most.

7

APPRAISING PERFORMANCE

After defining informally (and even sketchily) the employee's job expectations, the supervisor must appraise performance in relation to those expectations. As a practical matter, these two operations may be done line by line—that is, by writing down one job expectation and appraising performance of that, then another job expectation, and so forth.

QUANTIFYING APPRAISAL

How should this be done? On a scale of 1 to 10? A scale of 1 to 5? With an array of adjectives—poor, fair, good, excellent?

Experience with scales of numbers or words suggests that they beg the question of appraisal. Suppose we have decided that one of our job expectations for Joe, the shop foreman, is that he keep his people happy. Now we will try to estimate the degree to which he succeeds. How happy are his subordinates? Well, they range from one grouch at the outer edges of despair to a cheery soul who lives close to ecstasy. Clearly, we are trying to make a judgment that is beyond us.

What we should be trying to form a judgment on, in this case, is not how happy Joe's people are, but whether his efforts to maintain harmonious relations and conditions are getting satisfactory results. There may be some measurable elements that could help: the level of productivity of the work unit, the amount of absenteeism, the number of grievances and complaints. Taking such measures into account, we can form a judgment that Joe's results in "keeping his people happy" are either satisfactory or not. In any case, we abandon the attempt to estimate the *degree to which* he does this successfully.

So we vote for a simple on/off, yes/no, satisfactory/ unsatisfactory kind of summary judgment for each item on the list of job expectations. Scales, for this purpose, are difficult to manage and do not help appraisers reach the conclusions they must reach.

THE PROCESS OF APPRAISAL: A SECRETARY

For a view of the processes a supervisor might go through to appraise employee performance, let us follow through the expectations of a secretary that were suggested in the last chapter. Recall that they were:

> Being on hand, not late or absent or elsewhere
> Accuracy in typing
> Filing
> Screening calls

Keep in mind that we do not have to apologize to anyone for setting such expectations. We are the boss, the secretary is our employee, and these are the things we expect.

At the same time, we must face up to the question of whether we have ever shared these expectations with our secretary. If these are our principal job specifications, our secretary ought to be the first to know them.

Many employees never find out for sure what their bosses really want. Not surprisingly, such employees have a hard time meeting their bosses' expectations.

How might we appraise the performance of our secretary against these expectations—assuming she knows what they are?

Being on Hand

We want our secretary on hand when we need her. Her absence from her desk could be caused by her lateness, by her absence from work, or by her leaving after reporting in. What hard data might we have in this matter?

Keeping adequate attendance records would enable us to know how often our secretary has been absent, when, for how long, and for what reason. This record of attendance is either satisfactory or not. If it is an accurate record, it is objective fact. The productivity of an absent employee, whether the absence is one minute or one week, is zero. "Good" reasons for absence do not raise productivity.

The matter of being away from her desk is probably not documented, but it can be. If it comes to our attention that this is a problem, we could keep a simple record for a day or two of the number of times we needed our secretary and she was unavailable. Suppose it turned out to be 40 percent of the time. Is this satisfactory?

In the course of looking into this subject, we may well have to ask ourselves how often the secretary's being away from her desk is the result of our own orders. Do we send her to get coffee, pick out birthday cards, take papers to central typing, or bring in visitors from the lobby? Before we make a judgment about an employee's unsatisfactory performance in some respect, we need to be sure that we (or others) are not the cause of it.

Accuracy in Typing

Once we've jotted down the expectation that accuracy in typing is important to us, we need to examine what we mean. Presumably by accuracy we mean getting it right the first time and not having to type things over. If so, there are two skills involved: typing and proofing. What we are judging is the work that we see and the errors and inaccuracies that are in the copy when we see it. We have a right and indeed an obligation to draw conclusions about the quality of typing we see at that stage. It is presumably finished work at that point. Is it usually acceptable? What kinds of inaccuracies make it unacceptable?

We need to bear in mind that the level of perfection we expect may not always be attainable. So as we form summary judgments we need to ask what the probability is of getting someone who would do substantially better work. We do not have to settle for sloppy work, but we may have to be content with something less than perfection.

Filing

A number of questions may be raised about filing. Is it done promptly? Is the filing system adhered to? Can items be retrieved promptly? Can a person unfamiliar with the office use the system to find things?

Only when we have specified our expectations about filing to our own satisfaction can we appraise our secretary's performance in this respect. If we know what we mean, it will be easy.

Screening calls

Screening is partly a function of being there to intercept our calls. And when she is there, what is it we expect? Callers dealt with courteously and promptly? No inside secrets babbled? ("No, he isn't in *yet*.")

Certain callers judiciously deferred at certain times? Getting messages straight and conveying them in writing?

Screening can mean many things. What does it mean to us?

We need not take this appraisal example further to see that there is a definite pattern in appraising performance line by line against job expectations. The pattern goes like this:

- ☐ Does the employee know our job expectations? (If not, the appraisal *interview* should be devoted primarily to communicating them.)
- ☐ What precisely do we mean by the job expectations we wrote down?
- ☐ What objective measures do we have to help us make a summary judgment?
- ☐ To what extent are we or other people responsible for unsatisfactory performance?
- ☐ Is it possible that our expectations are unrealistically high?
- ☐ Is performance (line by line) satisfactory or not?

Once we have answered the above questions for each item on the list, we should have a set of notes something like the one below (S = satisfactory; U = unsatisfactory).

Being on hand: U—8 absences in last 7 months
Accuracy in typing: S
Filing: S
Screening calls: U—Inept handling when caller is to be deferred; apology overdone

THE OVERALL APPRAISAL

Given such a mixed rating, we must come to an overall conclusion. We must make a summary judgment of summary judgments. We must, in short, decide whether, all told, this subordinate's performance at this time is satisfactory.

Is such a harsh judgment really necessary? It is, because as we shall see the whole strategy of the appraisal interview depends on such a judgment. In our desire to avoid making such a harsh generalized judgment, we must keep in mind that we are not going to declare an employee's performance satisfactory or unsatisfactory to the president of the company. We are not, in fact, going to declare it to anyone. It is simply a fundamental decision we must make in order to make other decisions in turn.

Consider this logic: If an employee's performance is not satisfactory, we must consider whether he should be kept on the payroll. On the other hand, if his performance is satisfactory, we must ask ourselves about future promotion. The function of the appraisal process is to deal with future performance; thus the content and strategy of the interview depend on this fundamental satisfactory/unsatisfactory judgment.

How, then, do we arrive at such a conclusion? As a general rule, if any item on our list of job expectations has been appraised "unsatisfactory," we should appraise the employee's performance as a whole in the same way. This may seem a harsh approach, but it is based on the fact that the first order of business is to correct performance deficiencies on the current job. This does not mean that an employee's performance must be perfect in order to be satisfactory. It does mean that, in those few major expectations the supervisor has informally listed for appraisal purposes, there should be no performance less than satisfactory. In general, it is in the best interests of both the employee and the organization that all important performance deficiencies be corrected. Important to whom? To the boss.

Unsatisfactory Performance

Under the method of appraisal outlined here, the performance of many employees will end up in the "unsatisfactory" column. So we will consider that probability first. When the performance of an employee is judged less than satisfactory, a new question is raised: Can the deficiencies be corrected? This question must now be answered, because the course of the appraisal interview depends on it.

It unsatisfactory performance is judged correctable, the logical strategy is to find a way to get corrections going. If it is not correctable, only one fundamental decision remains: Fire the employee or resolve to live indefinitely with unsatisfactory performance. In any case, there is no reason to hold an appraisal interview with an employee whose performance is unsatisfactory and beyond correction. Nothing will be accomplished by such a meeting.

Thus the appraisal itself shapes the objective of the subsequent interview. Appraisal of unsatisfactory performance, when correctable, produces an interview objective of finding and agreeing on a way to correct deficiencies. (When performance is not correctable, the objective is not to have an interview!)

Some readers will stumble over the judgment of correctable/uncorrectable, but this need not be. Unsatisfactory performance is uncorrectable only if a person lacks the capacity or the desire to improve. Since both of these are easy to underestimate, the supervisor should usually err on the side of optimism and give it a try. Uncorrectable deficiencies become obvious when, after several attempts to obtain correction, the situation is no better. Of course, the number of futile attempts should be limited, but the supervisor should never make the mistake of throwing an employee on the bone pile too early. People have more resources than we usually imagine.

Satisfactory Performance

When performance on the current job is appraised as satisfactory, there is yet another decision. Some employees will be eligible for promotion, and for them appraisal interviews can be converted to *development interviews,* with emphasis on preparation for greater responsibility.

But promotion is not ahead for everyone. Sometimes the incumbent has already risen to his maximum level of achievement and would not be successful in a bigger job. Sometimes the employee is too close to retirement, or there are no jobs to promote him into, or his experience or education is not enough to qualify him for higher positions. In any case, the employee is doing satisfactory work at his present level and needs to be encouraged to continue doing so. This is generally true of most civil service employees. They become eligible for promotion not by satisfactory performance but by scoring high on competitive examinations. Their supervisors, therefore, must treat them as if they were ineligible for promotion because, in usual terms, they are ineligible.

So satisfactory performance, too, is treated in two ways. When promotion lies ahead, emphasis shifts from the present job to preparation for a future job. When promotion does not lie ahead—for whatever reason—the objective is to maintain current performance. The table shown here summarizes the principal outputs of appraisal.

Summary of Performance Appraisal		Future		Interview Objective
Satisfactory	→	Promotion	→	Make development plans
	↘	No Promotion	→	Maintain performance
Unsatisfactory	↗	Correctable	→	Plan correction
	↘	Uncorrectable	→	Fire or tolerate (No interview)

8

PLANNING THE INTERVIEW: UNSATISFACTORY PERFORMANCE, CORRECTABLE

When unsatisfactory performance is correctable, the objective of the interview is quite simple: to obtain improvement or correction. There is no concern with development for future promotions. The appraisal of performance against the supervisor's expectations has disclosed areas of unsatisfactory performance, and now the objective is to improve or perfect performance on the present job.

The simplicity of the objective does not make it easy to achieve. This is the most difficult of the three types of appraisal interviews and requires the greatest skill. The questions raised by such an objective include:

□ Should the supervisor try to gain improvement in all deficient areas or limit his objectives to a few?
□ If the objectives are to be limited, which should be chosen?
□ Will the employee accept his need to improve?

☐ If the employee may not readily accept the need to change, how can the supervisor best influence him?
☐ How much improvement is enough?

Such questions form the basis for planning the appraisal interview. The supervisor cannot enter such an encounter without raising such questions and planning the strategy of the interview.

SHOULD OBJECTIVES BE LIMITED?

An employee who is deficient in one or two areas can probably take them on and make progress before the end of the next appraisal period. If there are three or four specific areas for improvement, it may be too much to expect that all can be corrected in six months or a year. Loading the employee with several tasks of improvement may be counterproductive, leading only to low accomplishment, discouragement, and possibly poorer performance than already demonstrated.

Still, there is no reason to stretch performance improvement over a long period if it can be accomplished in a short time. An employee who can make dramatic gains should be challenged to make them; intentional foot-dragging is not in his or the organization's interest.

To deal with such questions, the supervisor must make some estimate of what the employee wants to do and is capable of doing. A marginal employee of relatively low motivation and ability may have to be groomed patiently into acceptable productivity over a long period. An employee who tries hard and/or has more ability can accomplish more growth in less time.

In summary, for some employees improvement can be accomplished in relatively little time. For others improvement must be undertaken in small increments. Most supervisors will know the difference and be able to adjust objectives accordingly.

SELECTING LIMITED OBJECTIVES

There are some useful criteria for selecting areas for performance improvement when it is unreasonable to expect that all can be attacked at once.

Is the deficiency critical? If an employee is in danger of losing his job unless he corrects a deficiency promptly, that deficiency has top priority. For example, an unsatisfactory attendance record or drinking on the job could lead to an employee's dismissal. If such a matter is on the supervisor's list of deficiencies, attention should be concentrated on it, because if it is not corrected none of the others will matter anyway.

Does the employee lack confidence? When an employee lacks confidence in his ability to do the job right, improvement efforts should be directed to those areas most likely to yield results. In short, concentrate on the easy ones first. Once the employee proves to himself that he can improve and succeeds at it, he will be more ready to tackle harder challenges. If he begins with a hard one and fails, he will only reinforce his belief that he can't make it.

Can improvements be laid end to end? The appraisal interview should not be the only time when performance improvement is discussed. The supervisor can make a "deal" with the employee for raising one deficiency to "satisfactory" over the next month and then tackling another deficiency at that time. It is a question not of limiting one's objectives within an appraisal period, but of spreading them out over the calendar year so that progress occurs continually.

ACCEPTING THE NEED TO IMPROVE

One of the most common errors of supervisors is to assume that any performance deficiency will be readily recognized and accepted by the subordinate. Such supervisors approach an appraisal interview expecting to get instant recognition of performance deficiencies and a hearty resolve to correct them. They are often surprised to find that employees do not readily accept the judgments of their superiors, do not accept the need to improve, and leave the interview rejecting judgments about poor performance, with no plan for improvement.

As we will see in later chapters, this kind of response often occurs when the supervisor begins with a false assumption and then magnifies the problem with a heavy-handed presentation of the employee's faults. But even when this error is avoided, the supervisor cannot be sure that the employee will see the need for change and accept the challenge. In fact, most of the time it is safer to assume that the employee will not quickly accept judgments about poor performance. Recognizing that possibility, the supervisor must plan the interview to lead the employee to see the need for improvement.

How is this done? What comes to mind to many supervisors first is that they gain the acceptance of a subordinate by the power of their office. Having (usually) the power to hire and fire, the supervisor relies on his authority and the threats implied by it to force compliance by the subordinate. The question of whether the employee will accept his judgments does not enter the supervisor's mind.

But we must recognize that compliance is not necessarily acceptance. In order to prepare the employee to perform as wholeheartedly as he can, the supervisor must do more than merely threaten him into meeting minimum requirements. In the arsenal of supervision, obtaining compliance under duress should be the last weapon.

Ideally, employees would come into appraisal interviews, state the ways in which their performance is deficient, and resolve to correct the situation. Some employees actually do this, but supervisors can hardly count on it. Thus taking a position somewhere between forcing compliance and waiting for the employee to announce his deficiencies is a productive middle ground.

In general, the employee should be encouraged to talk about specific areas of performance and to recognize that his performance needs improvement. When he has gone that far, planning the way for improvement is a natural and painless next step. The point is that the best results are obtained when the *employee states* that improvement is needed. Problems arise when the supervisor makes the statements and puts the employee on the defensive.

The following excerpts from appraisal interviews illustrate the contrast (**S** = supervisor, **E** = employee):

Appraisal 1
S: We've talked about your attendance record several times. What's your opinion about it?
E: Well, I guess it's not too great.
S: How important do you think it is to correct it?
E: I suppose I could lose my job if I didn't.
S: You're right, you could. What steps do you plan to take to make sure that doesn't happen?
E: Well, I've been having a lot of car trouble and that hasn't helped, but I'm getting a better car. . . .

Appraisal 2
S: You haven't made quota two of the last four quarters. It looks to me as if you just can't hack it.
E: I think you're jumping to a conclusion. Don't forget that. . . .
S: I'm not jumping to anything. I read your weekly reports and I just can't believe it. Most days you'd do better to stay in bed.
E: What do you think I'm doing wrong?
S: Doing wrong? You're just not selling, that's what's wrong. Anybody can see that.

The second supervisor's approach is wrong in so many ways that it is hard to begin correcting it. But it is clear that the supervisor will have a hard time getting any commitment to performance improvement out of the subordinate. By contrast, the first supervisor quickly leads the employee to recognize a problem and its possible consequences, and to begin talking about ways to improve.

Later on, we will take up the specific skills involved in making this kind of progress in an appraisal interview.

HOW MUCH IMPROVEMENT IS ENOUGH?

When performance is unsatisfactory but correctable, the objective of the interview is to get the employee to commit himself to and plan for improvement. But if the interview is to be successful, the extent of improvement needs to be specified.

An employee who is absent five times a month and then is absent only four times a month has clearly improved his attendance record. Is that what we mean by "improvement"? Probably not. First, we must make a clear distinction between improvement and correction. An employee can improve performance and still fall far short of satisfactory results. Correction, on the other hand, suggests virtual elimination of what is unsatisfactory.

In general, if you are dealing with matters of great urgency or seriousness, correction should be the objective. If improvement is a satisfactory goal, then the amount of improvement you expect should be quantified. How much improvement is expected? Meet quota every time? Produce 20 more units a day? Reduce the reject rate to .5 percent? Before you go into an appraisal interview, have some idea of how much improvement you are aiming for. During the interview you may want to negotiate the degree of improvement up or down, but you certainly should begin with at least a ballpark estimate of where you want the employee to go.

SUMMARY

An appraisal interview aimed at correcting unsatisfactory performance involves at least four basic decisions:

☐ Whether improvement will be sought in all deficient areas.
☐ Which objectives will be selected if all deficiencies are not included.
☐ How to lead the employee to accept the need for improvement.
☐ How much improvement to seek.

9

PLANNING
THE INTERVIEW:
SATISFACTORY
PERFORMANCE,
NO PROMOTION AHEAD

If the hardest interview is one aimed at performance improvement, the most poignant is one aimed at the employee whose work is satisfactory but who has little chance of promotion. Such an interview is probably the second most difficult, and for some supervisors it will be the most difficult of all.

Promotion does not lie ahead for every employee for a wide variety of reasons. Sometimes there are simply no vacancies and a low probability that any will develop. At other times an educational or other qualification stands as a barrier to promotion. Some jobs are stagnant simply by tradition; no one has ever been promoted out of them. Some employees have reached the limits of their abilities and cannot handle a bigger job; some would not accept a promotion if one were offered.

There are two kinds of people for whom promotion does not lie ahead: those who already know and accept the low probability of promotion, and those who either don't know it or don't accept it. Naturally, employees in the latter group are harder to work with in an interview, since they are less likely to be happy on their current assignment.

Included in the latter group in most organizations are people who should be promoted but who will not be. Most of these, if they are young enough and aggressive enough, will not be persuaded to be content with their present jobs. Supervisors have little hope of retaining such people. They are destined to rise, and if they do not do so in one organization they will do it in another.

One complication in this kind of interview is that many supervisors have little or nothing to say about the promotion of subordinates. Some, in fact, have no idea whether a particular employee can look forward to promotion. (In such a case, the supervisor will have to assume that promotion is possible.)

The supervisor's limited control over promotions is not always understood by subordinates. It is easy, for example, for an employee to have a favorable appraisal and an interview slanted toward development for a better job, and then to assume erroneously that promotion is definitely in the offing. If the supervisor were the one giving out promotions, this might be a safe assumption. But an immediate superior may have little or nothing to do with promotion. An employee who does not understand that and who is in danger of assuming too much should be informed of the truth. Good performance is not, for many reasons, assurance of promotion.

THE OBJECTIVE

When a subordinate is doing satisfactory work but has no prospect for promotion, there is no particular need to improve performance. Since development for an unlikely promotion would be a cruel hoax, the only objective for the appraisal interview is to maintain performance at the present level. This is a very worthy goal and a challenging one for the appraising supervisor. If no attempt is made to maintain satisfactory performance, the employee may eventually "run out of steam" and perform less effectively—or quit. The good supervisor, anticipating that possibility, works to avoid it.

What will maintain satisfactory performance? The wisdom of an earlier day holds that a man or woman is lucky to have a job and thus should extend his or her best efforts to keep it. A later and somewhat more sophisticated view recognizes that motivations change and that as one need is met, people begin reaching for a higher one. If this is true, we are on dangerous ground when we assume that an employee will continue to do good work indefinitely because he gets a check regularly and is covered by fringe benefits.

Once employees earn enough to meet the necessities of life, they shift their concern to their own safety and security. If their jobs fill these needs too, they turn their attention to social needs such as those for status and recognition. And when these are filled, they seek what may be called self-fulfillment. Thus the question of what motivates an employee must be answered in light of the person's immediate unfilled needs.

Not surprisingly, the most difficult needs to meet are the highest ones. The employee who makes a good salary, has a secure position, and enjoys high status in the corporate pecking order will seek to fulfill himself in the highest sense. And more than a few turn to a whole new occupation to realize such a goal. Relatively few jobs offer such a promise—at least, not in this life.

Thus when we try to find the "formula" for retaining a satisfactory employee who has no prospect of promotion, we need to know just what kinds of needs are being met. We can then try to meet the next higher set of needs. Chances are, a raise in pay or a few more fringe benefits will not do the job, because people's basic needs, including that for security, are already being met. People will be seeking recognition or status, and their continued good work on the job may depend on whether they find it.

A REPERTORY OF MOTIVATORS

One danger in even suggesting possible motivators to some supervisors is that they will seize upon them as gimmicks and attempt to motivate by manipulation. Most people know when they are being manipulated, and the illegitimate use of legitimate motivators is short-lived and ineffective. But the manipulator doesn't learn and continues to seek out gimmicks for using people to his advantage.

Despite this danger, we can suggest some techniques that can be helpful. They are not infallible, for people's response to them is not wholly predictable.

Appraisal itself may, at least for a time, encourage some good performers to continue as they are. Appraisal, whether formal or informal, supplies necessary feedback to the employee. It tells him that his work meets the boss's expectations. Appraisal cannot function in this way indefinitely, but it is certainly a positive step. Kind words too, no matter how sincerely intended, will not motivate forever. Most people need to feel there is some substance behind the occasional assurance "You're doing a good job." Insincere flattery, yet another form of manipulation, is also not part of the repertory of effective supervisors.

Delegation to a subordinate may be motivating. This does not mean heaping more tasks on him; there is nothing motivating about that. Rather, delegation is the transfer of some of your *authority* to a subordinate —having him do something that you normally do and using your authority or making the decisions instead of you.

Job enrichment—stretching a job to provide greater challenges to the incumbent—has much in common with delegation. The difference is that (1) the additional challenges are permanent, and (2) the enrichments may be drawn from others' work as well as your own, or from previously unmet organizational needs.

Participation is yet another way to meet people's needs for recognition and fulfillment by allowing them a say in decisions. There are limits to it, because an organization cannot be operated as a pure democracy with a vote taken on every decision. But individuals and groups can usually be given larger shares in decision making, for the good of the organization and themselves.

When you are preparing for an appraisal interview with a subordinate whose satisfactory performance you wish to continue, review this small repertory of motivators to find ways in which the person's current job can be made more satisfying to him. It may not be necessary to announce any such plans in the interview itself. If such enhancements come up later, they will add substance to the reassuring words you spoke in the interview.

WHEN THE EMPLOYEE "DOESN'T KNOW"

Some employees who are performing satisfactorily do not know that a promotion is improbable. Should they be told? Does the supervisor even know which employees are anticipating promotion when in fact they are unlikely to get one?

To answer the latter question first, we can state categorically that if a supervisor doesn't know whether an employee expects to be promoted, he doesn't know him well enough. The first order of business is to correct that deficiency.

Should an employee be told? Informing the subordinate is certainly in keeping with the rule of leveling with employees. But the supervisor must recognize his own limitations in predicting, as well as protect the feelings of his subordinate. Consider this case in which the employee's educational level bars the way to promotion:

S: As you know, Joan, the policy here is that people without a college education don't get above the first-line supervisor position. Now I don't know whether that policy will ever be changed, but as things stand now you would have to go to night school and pick up a degree to move up to the next level. Have you given any thought to that?

Or the case of an employee who has reached the probable limits of his ability on his current job:

S: You've come a long way in this job, Mike, and you handle it really well. Have you given any thought to the future and whether you want to try for another job?

E: Not very much, really. Do you think I should?

S: I think your first responsibility is to do the one you have just as well as you can. Then you need to consider what a bigger job would mean, and the scrambling you might have to do to get it and keep it. I would certainly caution you against getting in over your head—we've both seen good people get hurt that way. What's best for you and your family is to do what you know you can do.

E: You're right about that. I'm not sure I could handle a bigger job right now.

S: Well, if you feel like that, then certainly the thing to do is to make the best of this one.

None of these excerpts is intended to be a model. No one can provide words for you. But they do illustrate how supervisors can talk openly about difficult matters without shooting the employee down or handing him a vote of no confidence. Remember too that such conversations are held when a favorable appraisal is being discussed. It is a positive and supportive environment and a relatively easy one in which to deal with hard questions.

WHAT ABOUT THE APPRAISAL?

The comparison of the employee's performance with your own expectations, done before the interview, resulted in a rating of "satisfactory." It is easy enough to convey the details to the employee. The interview might start out like this:

S: Before we got together, I asked myself what I really expect of you on this job, and then I reviewed the way you handle the job in light of that. I'd like to just go over these things with you so you'll know how I feel about your performance and why. Now the first thing I considered was. . . .

Recall that this type of interview occurs only when you are generally satisfied with the employee's performance on the current job. You are not seeking performance improvement, so there are no important deficiencies to discuss. Rather, you want the employee to know what you expect and how well he meets those expectations, and you want to discuss the current job as he sees it. If the question of promotion has not already been resolved, you also need to deal with that. The interview, and your actions in day-to-day supervision after the interview, should lead to continued effective performance by the employee.

SUMMARY

In planning for this kind of appraisal interview, you should consider the following matters:

☐ The best way to work toward continued satisfactory performance on the current job.

☐ The needs you should try to meet at this time.

☐ Whether to employ delegation, job enrichment, participation, or other techniques.

☐ Whether the employee expects to be promoted, and if so, how to lower this expectation gently.

☐ The items in your formal appraisal that you want to share.

10

PLANNING THE INTERVIEW: SATISFACTORY PERFORMANCE, PROMOTION AHEAD

The easiest of the three types of appraisal interviews is one aimed at an employee whose performance is satisfactory and who is destined for promotion. Because there are no sensitive or controversial matters to be discussed, this interview is easy by comparison with the others. Nevertheless, skill is needed to conduct it effectively.

In a sense, such an interview is not an appraisal interview at all. Little time is spent on the appraisal itself, since improvement is not sought. The emphasis of the interview is on the employee's future—specifically, on preparing him for higher responsibility. Thus it is more aptly called a *development interview.*

A development interview is not without hazards. The most critical one is that the employee may interpret it as a promise of promotion, which, of course, it must not be. It is important, in fact, specifically to *deny* at the outset that promotion is assured.

Another hazard is possible conflict over the employee's goals. Asked how he sees his future, the employee may respond with a career pattern that seems wholly unrealistic to the supervisor. The skills discussed in Part II will help to avoid shooting down both the aspirations and the interview.

THE OBJECTIVE

When the employee is destined for promotion, the interview is intended to spur development for greater responsibility. It does not disregard performance on the current job, but neither does it emphasize it. Of course, if performance on the job has begun to slip, the employee and his supervisor should go back and concentrate on that. Development never overshadows current performance, but only supplements it.

Why should a supervisor spend time and effort preparing someone for another position? Why not wait until the position is vacant and then begin? One reason is that those who are destined to be promoted need to know it and prepare for it. A good employee who feels he has been forgotten may soon be someone else's employee. Another reason is that the employee who has had some preparation for greater responsibility can become productive faster when the time comes. Spending time and effort now may save time and effort later—and avoid some costly errors.

A final reason is that every progressive organization continually attempts to predict its future needs and to prepare people already on the payroll to fill them. To do otherwise is to run the danger that qualified people will not be on hand when vacancies occur, and selection will then have to be made among less than qualified people.

PLANNING—A SURVEY OF POSSIBLE SUPPORT

A supervisor who does not know the career plans of a subordinate cannot fully plan for this kind of interview. He will first have to discuss the subordinate's career plans with him, find out what they are, and then offer support. Thus planning will be more a review of possible support than a plan to commit such support.

The employee who wants to develop himself for greater responsibility must bear the principal burden. He must make his career plans, determine his development plans, and undertake the job of carrying them out. No one can do this for him. The role of the supervisor is to help in the process when possible. And unless the supervisor gives a good deal of attention to these matters regularly, he will have to do extensive preparation before he can discuss them intelligently.

Developmental steps can be taken in any one or all of three areas: on the job, within the organization off the job, and outside the organization.

On-the-job development includes personal coaching by the supervisor beyond the requirements of the current job. The subordinate could share, regularly or occasionally, tasks and responsibilities of the supervisor. He could have planned exposure to positions other than his own.

In-house, off-the-job development is limited to those developmental opportunities provided by the organization and could include company-sponsored courses, seminars, workshops, and conferences.

Development outside the organization has few limits. The subordinate could prepare for greater responsibility by reading, taking adult education or college courses, pursuing advanced degrees, or taking correspondence courses. Some organizations underwrite totally or partially such efforts at self-development.

SUMMARY

In planning for this kind of interview, you should follow these steps:

□ Review of supervisor's completed performance appraisal.

□ Discussion of subordinate's career plans and help in formulating them if needed.

□ Creation of specific plans for subordinate's development to be undertaken in the next appraisal period.

□ Commitment on the nature and extent of assistance to be given by the supervisor and/or the organization.

□ Review of developmental progress made since the previous interview if any had been planned then.

Part II

IMPROVING APPRAISAL INTERVIEWING SKILLS

11

AN INTRODUCTION TO INTERPERSONAL SKILLS

Appraisal interviews are just a couple of trees in the jungle of boss-subordinate relationships. Practically all this apparently impenetrable thicket can be accounted for by one fact: Most of us have difficulty rising above our limitations. We take our least desirable characteristics into relationships with others: spouses, children, superiors, subordinates. Then, when a storm threatens, we put up more sail instead of hauling in some of what's already out.

GETTING ALONG WITH OTHERS

As supervisors, managers, family heads, customers, and other interactors with people, we can learn something from psychologists, clergymen, psychiatrists, caseworkers, and others who spend a large portion of their time in one-on-one relationships. These people, too, have their weaknesses. They enter into relationships with the same pride, envy, jealousy, hostility, and defensiveness that plague the rest of us. Yet somehow most of them not only survive but manage to be respected and even loved by the people on the other side of the relationship.

The difference between the way these people handle relationships and the way most of us do can be accounted for by skill. There are teachable, learnable skills that help professional "people people" converse constructively. How else does a psychiatrist get a patient to tell how embarrassed she is to undress in front of her cat? How else does a clinical psychologist listen to a client's outpouring of sordid adventures without once exclaiming, "That's terrible." How else does a priest hear confessions?

"Getting along with people" is primarily talking and listening. Most of us can get along fine with others in nonverbal activities. It is when we start exchanging words that we lose first our cool and then our couth. If only we had some verbal skill—both in choosing the words we use and interpreting the ones other people use—we could do better.

Supervision and management are only beginning to be recognized as people-oriented jobs. Their history is of task orientation. Supervisors have long been thought of as being responsible for maintaining production, increasing sales, and so on, but only fleetingly as having much to do with people. Not surprisingly in such a climate, managers and supervisors have not been given any of the "people skill" training deemed essential for psychologists or caseworkers, for example.

That is beginning to change. As people come to be recognized as the principal assets of organizations, they may come to be managed as well as computers and assembly lines. Part of this management will include the communication of interpersonal skills.

PEOPLE SKILLS

The skills described in this part of the book are presented in the context of appraisal interviews. But they are not limited to that use. They are applicable to many situations with many kinds of people, for they are generalized "people skills." These skills are aimed at specific situations you may already have encountered in appraisal interviewing. For example, have you ever held an appraisal interview with a subordinate and discovered that you were doing most of the talking? Or have you ever tried, and failed, to get someone else talking? Does this dialog sound familiar?

S: How long have you been with us now, Harold?
E: Two years.
S: And how do you like it?
E: Fine.
S: Do you think you're doing a pretty good job?
E: I guess so.
S: Well, um, Harold, did you have a chance to go over the appraisal sheet?
E: Yes.
S: And, well, did you—did you see anything on there that you thought we ought to talk about?
E: No.

Not all employees are so laconic, to be sure, and when they're not, have you ever begun to wish that they had been?

S: You feel, then, that you were not very well trained for your present job?
E: Not very well! I wasn't trained at all. I spent two weeks sitting with a dummy downstairs in General Accounts who couldn't add 5 and 3 without a calculator, and at the end of that time he was fired. Then you put me in Accounts Receivable without a word of instruction, and the first week the only thing I found out was the guy at the next desk had been embezzling since 1943. Maybe you call that training, but I'd rather go over Niagara Falls in a barrel. Some outfit this is!

Now how do you respond to all that? How do you keep the subordinate from becoming defensive and hostile? How do you keep yourself, for that matter, from becoming defensive?

Even if you are able to maintain a climate of sweetness and light during the interview, there is always the possibility that it will come to naught. It takes skill to direct the interview, accomplish its purposes, stay on the subject, and get the job done. Without this skill, you can preside over a lot of very nice chats that accomplish nothing. The skills you read about in the following chapters are essential to effective appraisal interviewing and useful in other areas of your business and private life too. They will help all your interviews achieve their objectives.

12

GETTING
THE SUBORDINATE
TALKING

There is good reason for calling discussions of personnel appraisals "interviews" and not "lectures." Supervisors do not bring subordinates into a room one by one and try to effect change by lecturing to them. To be sure, a lot of supervisors have tried that, but they have not been very successful. Before going on, we should understand why.

The objective of many appraisal interviews is, quite properly, to bring about some change in an employee's performance. A casual look at the situation suggests that the supervisor is in an excellent position to do this. He has authority to give orders, perhaps to hire and fire, to recommend pay raises, to suspend, to lay off. From his seat of authority, he should theoretically be able simply to *order* improvement.

But despite the amount of authority we seem to have as supervisors, we have little ability to get people to do things they really don't want to do. This is more true of the *way* employees do things than of the tasks themselves. The way people function is somehow part of them, and they do not change easily.

Resistance to change is stiffened when the person in authority sits in judgment, calls the shots, orders the changes, and relies on his authority to effect them. Resistance is somehow softened when people are encouraged to air their opinions and feelings about their work.

THE RATIO OF TALKING TO LISTENING

The probability that an appraisal interview will accomplish its purposes is directly related to the amount of talking done by the subordinate. The ratio of the subordinate's input to the total has been measured by recording the interview, transcribing it, and counting words. In interviews that show real promise of accomplishing their purposes, the supervisor speaks only about 10 percent of the total words in the interview. As the supervisor's proportion of words goes up, the success of the interview is reduced. The least successful interviews show the supervisor dominating the conversation.

As a general rule, then, the appraisal interview should involve eight or nine times as much talking by the subordinate as by the boss. This rule holds, not because subordinates know more than their bosses, but because the ratio is directly related to the probable success of the interview. In most interviews, success may be measured by the subordinate's acceptance of his need to improve his performance in some significant way. In this situation bosses are agents of change, trying to get the employee to do most of the talking.

CHANGING THE RATIO

If you already do only about 10 percent of the talking in appraisal interviews, you must count yourself among the elite. Most supervisors tend to dominate conversations with their subordinates—not just appraisal interviews, but all conversations.

You don't have to wait until the next appraisal interview to find out about your own practices. Just try to "tune in" on the next few conversations you have with subordinates and see who does more talking. (You will find yourself trying *not* to dominate such conversations even as you monitor them!)

There are two, and only two, things you can do to change the ratio of talking to listening. One is passive: keeping quiet. The other is active: eliciting talk from the other person. Psychologists and counselors become expert at both.

Expert at keeping quiet? What kind of expertise is that? Anyone can keep his mouth shut. But as you look at the experience of parents with their children, teachers with their pupils, and bosses with their subordinates, you are likely to conclude that it is a wise person indeed who knows how and when to keep his mouth shut.

Imagine two people coming together for an appraisal interview and staring at each other in silence for half an hour. It is highly unlikely that such a thing would occur. If it did, of course, the interview would be a disaster. But would it be any worse than the following?

S: I've analyzed your performance very carefully and I can see you've got a long way to go. You know, I've seen a lot of people come and go, and when you've been around as long as I have you can just tell who's going to make it in this business and who isn't. Now you've got a lot going for you, but you're about as aggressive as a fat mouse, and if there's anything that will keep someone from succeeding, it's a lack of aggressiveness. I remember when I started out back in 1942. My boss said to me, "You know, Charlie, if it wasn't for the war and the manpower shortage I never would have hired you, but you're aggressive and that's going to carry you through even without the other things I wish you had.'' And he was right, wasn't he?

E: Yep.

S: He was right, wasn't he? All these other hot shots have come and gone, and old Charlie's still here, meeting his district quota every month, right?

E: Right.

S: Right?

E: Right.

The overwhelming conclusion we must reach here is that old Charlie said absolutely nothing that could not have been improved on by silence.

To refrain from talking is at least to *enable* the other person to talk. The employee may not do so. He may clear his throat, roll his eyes, and wish he were on Madagascar. But the chances that he will speak when you do not are infinitely greater than the chances that he will interrupt or override you while you are speaking. Most of us would rather do the talking, but we have been taught that it is impolite to talk when another is speaking, especially if he is the only other person there.

THE VALUE OF SILENCE

The creative use of silence is a valuable skill, well known and used in clinical practice. Sometimes silence is the best tool to get or keep another person talking, as in this example:

E: I've really come to hate my job. I mean, I really hate the thought of coming to work in the morning.

S: *(Silence.)*

E: Actually, of course, I don't hate it all that much. It's really the sameness of a lot of it that gets to me. But there are times when—when I actually get a kick out of it. Like last week, when that electroplating project came in the shop. . . .

What a great temptation most of us would have to talk when an employee tells us he hates his job. Our urge to be helpful, judgmental, or authoritative would lead us to cut off such a flow of feelings with contributions like these:

□ "After all I've done for you, you sit there and tell me you hate your work?"
□ "What do you mean, you hate to think of coming to work? If you feel that way you'd better start looking for another job."
□ "If I felt that way about my work, I think I'd slit my throat. You shouldn't feel that way."

What the thoughtful supervisor did in this case, however, was to make no response at all. In the pause that followed, the employee felt that he was free to go on talking and recognized that he had really overstated his case. He tempered his position. He didn't really hate his job that much. It was the sameness he hated. And there were really some enjoyable aspects of it.

From this and indeed literally thousands of other experiences in trying to converse constructively with others, we can make some obvious but important observations about the uses of silence.

Silence almost never offends. While almost anything anyone says could be seen as offensive under some circumstances, silence is gloriously neutral. It calls for no rebuttals, defenses, or new evidence.

Silence is a verbal cathartic. Most people are unable to tolerate silence for long. If two people are in a room together and one is silent, the other will feel a compulsion to say something, if only to fill the silence. If you want someone to speak, keep quiet, and before many seconds have elapsed he will.

Silence is nonjudgmental. Most people are careful of what they say because they expect to be judged. When a subordinate tells you he hates his job and would rather be on welfare than work another day, and you respond with silence, he will be greatly relieved at your failure to make a judgment. If you aren't more careful with your silences, he may even wind up thinking you're a nice guy!

The ability to use silence creatively and constructively is a valuable tool. You can learn from a book how valuable it is in theory. In practice, you will learn a lot more. The hard part is to get the practice—that is, to keep your mouth shut long enough to see the effect it has.

Begin by being aware that you probably do most of the talking in the company of an employee. Monitor your conversations consciously and find out if it's true. If it is, try substituting some very brief, noncommital responses for the lectures you may be prone to give. None of these qualifies as absolute silence, but all of them come close: "Uh-huh," "Yes," "I see," "Mm-hm," "Oh?" As you become aware of your tendency to dominate and make a conscious effort to substitute silence for talk, you will immediately begin to notice differences. They will start out as differences in the ratio of speaking to listening, but they will come to improve your daily relationships with subordinates.

THE USE OF QUESTIONS

Silence is the vacuum into which the words of your subordinate will be drawn. Your silence, to some extent, will actually elicit talk from others. But the limitations of silence as a tool for eliciting talk will quickly become obvious. People almost always move to fill silence with words. But when you are trying to direct an appraisal interview toward a specific goal, you need to do more than fill silences. To direct the talk to the objectives of the interview, you will need to ask questions. And if skill is involved in using silence, far more skill is involved in using questions to direct an appraisal interview.

Consider the interview excerpt you read in the last chapter. In response to five questions, the supervisor elicited the following:

"Two years."

"Fine."

"I guess so."

"Yes."

"No."

We could take the position that the employee was a man of few words. But if we look more closely at the questions the supervisor asked, we can see that they have a common defect. Here are the questions:

"How long have you been with us now, Harold?"

"And how do you like it?"

"Do you think you're doing a pretty good job?"

"Did you have a chance to go over the appraisal sheet?"

"Did you see anything on there that you thought we ought to talk about?"

The defect is that each question is so phrased that a short answer will suffice. In fact, each question appears to be asking for information. The employee obligingly provides it: two years, fine, he guesses so, yes, no. People ask questions like these because they have been taught that questions are used to gather information. What time is it? Where's my hat? Did the mail come? Where's Elmer?

What we must now learn is that the questions used in appraisal interviews are not intended to collect data. We use questions, not to get short, factual answers, but *to get the other person thinking and talking.* Only if we are successful in doing that can the interview effect change.

This means that you must be conscious, for perhaps the first time, of the *kind of responses* a question will get before you ask it. When you are seeking information, you just ask any old way, or so it seems, and you find out what you want. When you are trying to get a

person talking, a question may do the job or not according to the way you ask it.

This is not a matter of the *content* of the question. It
makes no difference whether you ask a question about
grapes, locomotives, or transactional analysis. It is the
form of the question that determines the extent of the
response. A question can be phrased to elicit a short
answer or to preclude a short answer. The trouble with
the questions in the struggling dialog we read earlier
was that they all permitted short answers, and that's
what they got.

In the next chapter we will take up three basic question types and find out how to use them to get the
responses we want.

13

TYPES OF QUESTIONS

At this point we are going to try to abandon our old habits of asking questions to get information. Instead, we will attempt to develop a new use for questions: to get another person talking. In a sense, we will formulate questions according to the flow of words we hope they will generate.

RESTRICTIVE QUESTIONS

Let's begin with the type of question with which we are most familiar: the kind we use to get information. This kind is the *least* useful in getting people to open up. The most common of these are questions that call for a yes-or-no answer—the kind used to play Twenty Questions. They often start out with the following:

"Did you . . ."
"Will you . . ."
"Can it . . ."
"Is it . . ."
"Has she . . ."
"Have you . . ."

What all these questions have in common, regardless of their content, is that they can be answered with a single word: "Yes" or "No." It is possible that they will get an equivocating answer, such as "I'm not sure" or "Could be," but these are not much more revealing than the "Yes" or "No" for which they substitute. It is also possible, of course, that a simple yes-or-no question will elicit a lengthy response. The point here, though, is that the question itself permits a short answer and to a large extent *restricts* the answer to a very few words.

Another type of restrictive question calls for short bursts of information and does little to get the respondent talking. Here are examples:

"How long have you been with us now, Harold?" ("Two years.")

"When did you leave?" ("4:30.")

"Where's my hat?" ("On the rack.")

"Who wrote this?" ("Joe.")

"What book is this?" ("*The World Almanac.*")

These restrictive questions do not elicit yes-or-no answers but neither do they go beyond the specific content asked for. Because they are so restrictive, they are of little value in getting people to talk. The questions are usually longer than the answers.

If we were limited to the repertory of restrictive questions at most people's command, our hopes of effective appraisal interviewing would be dim indeed. But fortunately, we need not be confined to a single kind.

OPEN-END QUESTIONS

At the opposite end of the spectrum is the open-end question. This form not only supplies plenty of latitude for the response but makes it difficult or impossible for the respondent to answer in a word or two.

"How do you feel about protective tariffs?"

"What could we do to reduce costs?"

"How do you account for this problem?"

"Why has this gone on so long?"

"What were your best courses in college?"

It is true that a person who is very reluctant to express himself could get out of such questions with a few words. For example:

"I'm opposed."

"I don't know of a thing."

"Got me."

"Nobody tried to stop it."

"English and German."

However, such questions usually do not elicit such short answers, particularly when the questioner makes it clear that he wants the other person to talk. Look at the following example, an alternative approach to interviewing our friend Harold.

S: How long have you been with us now, Harold?

E: Two years.

S: Well, that's long enough to give you a good view of your job. How do you feel about your job? (*Open-end*)

E: Fine.

S: What are the things you like best about it? (*Open-end*)

E: Well, I think probably dealing with the customers over the counter. I like to hear what their needs are, and then try to help them.

S: Mm-hm. (*Silence.*)

E: Of course, there are some customers who are hard to deal with, but most of them are nice, and they really seem to appreciate the help we give them. I guess that's what I like best—when the customer comes in needing help, and he gets it, and he goes away happy.

This is very early in the interview, and it is off to a good start. The boss has asked only three questions, one of them a bummer, but he has already elicited 80 words, compared with his own 38. (If you want to count his noncommital "Mm-hm," it's 39.) That gives the subordinate about 2 words out of every 3 spoken, and that's not a bad ratio for the early stages of the interview.

While it may seem trivial to be counting words and rendering judgments on the totals, we must recognize that getting the employee to do most of the talking is critical to the success of the interview. We must also be concerned with the *quality* and the *direction* of the conversation, but at the outset let's devote our attention to getting the employee talking and the supervisor listening.

OPEN-END PROBLEM QUESTIONS

A useful variation on asking an open-end question is posing a real or hypothetical problem and asking the employee how he would handle it. Such a device can be stimulating and reveal a good deal about the interviewee. Consider this problem question posed by a sales manager to a salesman. The supervisor is trying to get at the employee's ability to handle management problems, because he is considering recommending the salesman for promotion to management.

S: Suppose you were a sales manager and you had reason to believe one of your salesmen was falsifying some reports about his calls and expenses. How would you handle it? (*Open-end problem*)

E: Boy, that's a honey! Well, I think the first thing I'd do is try to make sure that what I suspected was really true. I'd have to do that very carefully, because if he *was* falsifying I wouldn't want him to get wise that I was suspicious. On the other hand, if he *wasn't* falsifying, he'd really be put down if he found out what I suspected. So I'd have to find out all I could very discreetly. Then, if I found that he was really falsifying, I'd just have to confront him.

S: What do you mean by that? (*Open-end*)

E: Well, I'd just have to lay it out for him and say, look, Bill, this is what's happening and I know all about it. And I guess I'd have to fire him.

S: Why? (*Open-end*)

E: I just don't see how I could do otherwise. It's not as if he made a mistake, you know, or lacked some skill that he could learn. If it were that, you could give him another chance. But if he has this, this character defect, and he cheats and falsifies the records, how could you ever trust him? I know it seems harsh, but I just don't see any other way to handle it.

The above dialog is presented not as a textbook solution to handling dishonesty, but as an example of using a problem question to elicit revealing thinking and talk from another. The technique is very simple: Pose a real or hypothetical problem and ask the employee how he would deal with it. More examples:

- "How would you do it if you were me?"
- "Suppose productivity declined by 1% every month for six months. What action would you take?"
- "I've got to find some way to keep these payroll costs down. What do you think I should do?"

These are really open-end questions which state a problem. They restrict the *content* of the response but not the words.

THE COMMAND

Also akin to the open-end question is an order or command to talk about something. Such commands are not barked out like "Forward, march!" but occur naturally in the course of conversation.

E: There was one time when I really felt I wasn't cut out for this kind of work.

S: Tell me about it.

The command is used in the same way as the open-end question, and it has the same effect on the other party. It says, "Tell me more," or "Keep talking," or "Give me some details." It's an encouragement to open up and places no restriction on the length of the response desired.

CHOICE QUESTIONS

We have dealt so far with two basic types of questions: the restrictive question and the open-end question. They represent opposite ends of the question range. The first gets short, factual answers; the second gets at attitudes, feelings, opinions, and other useful information about the person.

The last question type we will consider—the choice question—falls somewhere in between. It is more open than a restrictive question and less open than an open-end question. It is used as a stimulant, often to cover for a previous question that fails. In the following example, the open-end question fails because it is too broad for the other person.

S: What fears do you have about your job? (*Open-end*)

E: Fears? I don't know that I have any fears.

S: Well, I mean things like security, or being able to do it right, or wondering if you won't get bored with it someday. (*Choice*)

E: I see what you mean. I used to worry, in the early days, about being able to do it right, but I don't think about that much any more. I guess what I really wonder about these days is what's ahead for me.

In the above dialog, the boss used a perfectly good open-end question that just didn't seem to register. The subordinate's second response, "I see what you mean," shows clearly that he hadn't understood the first question. The second, by way of clarification, listed three possible "fears" or "worries." The subordinate chose one from the list that he once worried about but no longer did. And that led him to express a current concern.

A choice question, then, provides two or more options from which the respondent may select.

The advantage of such a question is that it stimulates the respondent either to select one of the offerings or to come up with his own.

S: What are the things you like best about your job? (*Open-end*)

E: Oh, I don't know.

S: Well, is it the people, or the tasks, or the pay, for instance?

E: It's not the pay, that's for sure. No, I guess I'd say it's the people. I really like working with Jerry and Sue and those people.

This response leaves the boss with two subjects to pursue. He got a negative response on the pay, and he can probe that one. Or he can pursue the positive response about working with people. The one he chooses will, of course, be determined by the objectives of the interview.

The choice question, then, falls between the restrictive and the open-end questions in terms of its ability to "open up" the respondent. It helps the respondent to be specific, opens up new areas for discussion, and clarifies previous questions that were either too broad or too narrow.

COMBINATIONS

The effective appraisal interviewer is not a Johnny One Note who selects his favorite question type and uses that exclusively. It would never work. An effective interviewer uses the whole range of question types, mixing them expertly to achieve the objective he chose at the outset of the interview. He selects his question types from his repertory as the need arises, trying always to get the subordinate to talk more while he talks less. Consider the following dialog and the boss's use of a range of questions (a salesman and his manager).

S: How much thought have you given to your future? (*Open-end, not really calling for a quantified answer*)

E: Oh, not very much, I guess.

S: Well, have you decided whether you want to go into management, or stay in sales, or maybe get into product management? (*Choice*)

E: Oh, I've given some thought to product management, but I'm not sure I'd really like that.

S: What do you think you wouldn't like? (*Open-end*)

E: Well, first of all, I'm not sure I'd like working in that home office environment. There's all that pressure and politicking. And I would really miss working in the field—the customer contact and all that.

S: Would you like to find out more about it so you can make a better choice? (*Restrictive*)

E: I sure would.

S: All right. I'll set up an interview for you at the regional conference. Now what else can we be doing about your future? (*Open-end*)

E: Well, of course, the most obvious route is in sales management. That's the one most guys talk about: district manager, regional manager, and so forth.

S: How do you feel about that route? (*Open-end*)

E: Open-minded, I guess. It's a natural kind of progression, and it doesn't close the door on other kinds of openings later on.

S: You'd like to have an escape route? (*Restrictive*)

E: Well, I'm just not certain enough yet that I want to spend my whole life in sales. There are a lot of good things about it, and I haven't a complaint in the world. But I'm still not absolutely sure that selling and sales management are what I want from here to retirement.

The above is a sample of how question types must be mixed to move an interview toward its objective. The manager stayed quite open-ended, helping the salesman clarify his thinking about the future.

The judicious use of a range of question types is certain to elicit considerable verbal input from the employee. The question that now arises is how one should respond to such input—a topic we turn to in the next chapter.

14

RESPONDING TO
INPUT

As we have seen, the first task of the interviewer is to
elicit talk from the interviewee. It is not, of course,
just talk, but talk about matters of joint concern about
the employee's job, his performance, his problems,
and his future.

The only thing that will interfere with this process is
the supervisor's own responses. Given responses that
encourage the flow of words, the subordinate will keep
them coming. Given responses that divert or discour-
age, he will either take the conversation off the track
or stop altogether.

WHAT NOT TO SAY

Some responses by the supervisor will interrupt or
divert the process. These fall into six common catego-
ries, and the expressions may be all too familiar.

JUDGMENT:	You shouldn't have done that.
FREE ADVICE:	Now if I were you I'd take a course in night school.
NAME CALLING:	You stupid jackass.
RIDICULE:	Where'd you ever learn that?

DIVERSION: That reminds me of the time I
                      went hunting in Canada with my
                      brother-in-law.
SARCASM: I'd hoped you'd handle this thing
                      intelligently, but I suppose you
                      hate to break a perfect record.

We could make a much longer catalog of put-downs, squelches, irrelevancies, condemnations, and other verbal abuses to avoid in appraisal interviews, but it is hardly worth the trouble. Most of these blocks to effective communication arise out of one-upmanship, that endless game some of us play to convince ourselves that we are better than the next guy. They demonstrate uneasiness about ourselves, and they show clearly that it is very hard to be an effective boss when we are wrestling with our own hangups.

Once we recognize these kinds of responses for what they are, we can learn to keep them out of all conversations, with employees and otherwise. No textbook can possibly teach supervisors to do this. But supervisors can teach themselves to abandon such devices, which destroy good communication.

SILENCE AND NONVERBAL COME-ONS

We have already noted the creative use of silence to stimulate conversation on the part of the employee. Silence is especially effective when it is used as a response to the words of another. This does not mean that questions can be ignored, shocking statements passed over, and a general sphinx posture assumed. It does mean that you should not feel obligated to respond orally line by line or whenever your subordinate pauses for breath.

Silence, because it does not interfere with the other person's talking, encourages him to continue. Silence can be made even more encouraging when it is accompanied by such simple nonverbal signs as smiling and nodding. These unobtrusive signals convey such messages as, "I understand, tell me more," or "I hear what you're saying and I'm offering no judgments, so keep it coming."

Your own silence not only leaves a vacuum to be filled by the other person; your own act of will in remaining silent also prevents you from uttering numerous no-nos to good interviewing—such as judgments, advice, and criticism. It may very well be that most skills involved in encouraging the verbal input of another lie in the use of silence and nonverbal signs. This may seem a great oversimplification of a complex battery of skills, but it would not be hard to prove that an interviewer who could only nod, smile, and keep his mouth shut could go a long way.

RESTATEMENT

Another not so simple device used by clinicians is the reflection of a subordinate's feelings, or *restatement*. In the following example of restatement, note that the feeling is being reflected back to the speaker, not the content.

E: The worst part of my job is filling out those miserable reports. I put that off just as long as I can.
S: You really hate doing it.
E: I sure do.

This neutral and seemingly unimpressive method of responding is actually a very powerful technique. When the supervisor says, "You really hate doing it," he:

□ Is telling the employee that he has been listening carefully.
□ Shows that he knows how the employee feels, and seems to care.

☐ Is not making any judgment about the employee's feeling; in fact, he seems to be very much on his side.

☐ Is approving of sharing such feelings and would seem to permit sharing other feelings as well.

Consider how encouraging and accepting this restatement response is in comparison with more typical responses from people:

E: The worst part of my job is filling out those miserable reports. I put that off just as long as I can.

ADVICE: You'd better learn to like 'em because you're going to be living with them a long time.

JUDGMENT: You have to respect the fact that the company needs those reports just to operate.

SARCASM: I thought you must be enjoying them, you linger over them so long after the deadline.

Restatement has more than a salutary effect on the listener. It takes intensive effort to hear what the other person is really saying, and the ability to separate feeling from content. It provides instant feedback on how well the listener understands, for any inaccurate reflection of feelings will be challenged.

E: I never had any experience with milling machines, but they put me in there and I just had to do the best I could.

S: You felt they shouldn't have put you in that job.

E: No, it wasn't that. But somebody should have given me some training before they did it.

You can practice the skill of restatement on virtually everyone you talk to: husband, wife, child, friend, associate, employee. It goes like this:

1. Listen intently. What is the other person really saying?
2. Separate feeling and content.
3. Respond to feeling with restatement, trying to reflect the feeling you think the other person is expressing.

The difficult part of restatement lies in separating the content from the feeling; it is easier and more natural to respond to content.

I hate maple walnut ice cream.

The content here is maple walnut ice cream. The feeling is strong dislike, distaste. The response, "So what's wrong with maple walnut?" would miss the feeling entirely. The message is "hate" and a correct restatement would be, "You don't like it one bit."

If an employee says, "I think the company vacation policy stinks," your response would not have to do with the vacation policy, but with his feeling about it.

Some people have trouble reflecting feelings because they are afraid they will appear to be agreeing with ideas or feelings they don't agree with. But agreement is not part of it at all. The mirror on the wall does not agree or disagree with your face; it simply reflects it back. That is what restatement does with feeling. It does not say, "I feel that way too," or "That is a good feeling and I approve." It just says, "This is what I understand your feeling to be. Is it correct?"

Practice for yourself by trying to restate the feelings contained in each of the following statements:

"I'm fed up to the ears working overtime and not getting paid for it."

"The chances of my getting promoted are really slim."

"It wasn't my fault that those mistakes were made."

"I'm sorry I ever took the job."

"What I like best is when I'm left on my own to develop and carry out a whole project."

The knowledgeable use of a range of question types will get all but the most reticent people talking. To keep them talking, you should:

1. Avoid judgmental responses.
2. Respond some of the time with silence.
3. Supplement silence with encouraging nonverbal signs like smiles and nods.
4. Restate feelings from time to time.

The skills described in the last chapter and this one will help create a flow of talk between subordinate and supervisor. In the next chapter we will discuss how to keep the appraisal interview on the track so that it is not just a flow of talk but a constructive conversation.

15

KEEPING ON
THE TRACK

As suggested in Part I, every appraisal interview has a preselected objective. To be successful, the interview must be directed to achieve that objective. Anything that may divert it from its objective is to be avoided.

The most common diversion in appraisal interviews aimed at getting improved performance is emotional interference. The sequence of events leading to this kind of diversion is predictable:

1. The supervisor tells the subordinate what is wrong with his performance.
2. The subordinate takes it as personal criticism and acts defensively.
3. The supervisor does not accept the defensiveness and in the process becomes defensive himself.
4. The interview goes off the track of reason and becomes an emotional exchange.

This process may be seen in the following excerpt from a well-intentioned interview:

S: I've been over your performance pretty carefully, Jim, and in a great many ways it's excellent. I think we'd probably get a lot more constructive work

done if we concentrated on some things where
maybe there could be some improvement.

E: O.K.

S: The thing I have in mind in particular is that tendency of yours to try to do everything at the last
minute rather than to plan things out. You know
what I mean?

E: I know I'm kept mighty busy around here and I
don't have much time for planning.

S: Well, excuse me, but I don't think that's a very
good excuse.

E: I'm not making excuses, I'm just telling you the
way it is. There's just no time for a lot of fancy
planning.

S: I'm not advocating a lot of fancy planning, Jim, I'm
just trying to tell you that you can't build a career
on management by crisis. You've got to control
events or they wind up controlling you.

E: That's good philosophy, Murray, but we just don't
have the kind of operation where that makes any
sense. You're forever putting the heat on me, and I
get the job done, don't I? And now you're saying I
don't, or you don't want it done on a crisis basis.
You're the one who creates the crises, not me. If
you would just—

S: Now don't be ridiculous, you know perfectly
well—

This interview began to go off the track in Murray's
second speech: ". . . that tendency of yours to try to
do everything at the last minute rather than to plan
things out."

Jim interpreted this as personal criticism and immediately became defensive. His defense was a reason
why he couldn't do more planning: "I don't have
much time for planning."

True as this may have been, Murray saw it as an

excuse and was quick to label it. Jim denied that it was an excuse and repeated it. This led Murray to get on the soapbox to do some preaching: "You've got to control events or they wind up controlling you."

This seemed to Jim to be still another personal criticism. Even more defensive now, he moved to transfer the blame: "You're the one who creates the crises."

By that time Murray had stopped listening and his own defenses were aroused. He interrupted Jim and overrode his speech with a new attack:

"Now don't be ridiculous."

This statement, equivalent to saying "You *are* being ridiculous," called for still another defense by Jim, some more defense by Murray, and additional exchanges of verbal blows. In only a few minutes the interview was completely derailed, and the best that could possibly come of it is a restoration of the conditions that existed before.

This dialog is not presented to frighten readers from facing up to subordinates' performance weaknesses. Rather, it is a demonstration that there is skill involved in the appraisal interview, and that if that skill is not learned and put to work, the interview will not succeed.

DIRECTING CONVERSATION TO THE JOB

The first task in appraisal interviewing is to focus the conversation on the job. Two people are involved, and when the conversation becomes a personal matter, as in the dialog above, the interview is threatened.

Well, some readers may say, isn't an employee's performance a personal matter? It is, of course, but if you and he are going to talk about it objectively, you will have to regard it as something outside both of you. The way to do this is to treat the job as the focus of the interview. The subordinate wants to get the job done and so do you. He wants to succeed and you want him to. The interview must, then, exploit the common interest that you and he have in the job.

The supervisor in the dialog above opened with a personal criticism: "... that tendency of yours...." Had he used the principle of joining with the employee to deal with the problem, he might have said many other things, all a good deal less threatening:

☐ "In our kind of work we have to strike a balance between getting today's work out and planning for future work."

☐ "I've been giving some thought to how we can improve our planning and avoid last-minute rushes. Do you have any thoughts on that?"

☐ "We've talked from time to time about doing better planning. How do you feel about the progress we've been making?"

All these examples—and many more could be cited— introduce the problem without making any direct accusations. The word "we" appears in each of them, suggesting that the supervisor wants to team up with the subordinate to attack the problem. Since there is no attack on the subordinate, he will not have to defend himself, and the attention and resources of both parties can be directed to the job.

In the example given here, a statement leads to discussion of a performance deficiency. But there may be occasions in the interview when redirection is needed. Redirection too should focus on the job rather than on the characteristics of the employee, as in this statement, for example: "We were talking about ways to improve productivity in the shop."

AVOIDING DEFENSIVENESS IN THE SUBORDINATE

We have considered the value of teaming up with the employee to solve a job problem. It eliminates the attack and thus the need for defense. Sometimes, though, despite our best efforts to avoid anything that can be interpreted as an attack, the subordinate becomes defensive. He may grope for excuses, blame others, or otherwise try to justify his actions or attitudes.

The worst response is to meet the defensiveness head on:

S: Your people are just not putting out well enough.

E: It's the best I can do with those dummies I've got working for me.

S: Those dummies are not the problem.

A response like this is almost certain to generate still higher levels of defensiveness. With that, the interview goes off the track, as increasing amounts of energy are spent in defense and correspondingly less in solving the problem.

Reassurance

One simple device for avoiding defensiveness is to offer reassurance. This involves taking a position at least in part on the defender's side, reducing his need to escalate his defense:

E: It's the best I can do with those dummies I've got working for me.

S: It's not easy to get really top performance out of them, is it?

E: It sure isn't—although sometimes I'm surprised at how well they work.

In this exchange, the subordinate's defenses are quickly deflated by a position of reassurance taken by the supervisor. Here is another:

E: I agree that we all have to be budget-conscious, but half my budget is mandated and I have no control over it at all.

S: So you really can't be held responsible for spending on that half of the budget, can you?

E: No.

S: We'll have to concentrate on those areas of budget-
ing and spending where you do have control, right?

E: Absolutely. I accept full responsibility for the
things I control.

This turned out to be a very positive exchange once
the question of the "mandated" part of the budget was
disposed of. Once he acknowledges responsibility for
what he controls, the subordinate can work within his
own declaration.

Again, it is the interviewer who holds the key to
such developments. It is he who introduces the topic
in a nonthreatening way, invites the input of the subordinate, and reduces his need to act defensively. The
technique of *reassurance* is one of several devices
used consciously by the interviewer to keep the interview on a productive track.

Restatement

We have seen how restatement or reflection of feelings
can help keep most of the input coming from the subordinate. This technique is also appropriate in the
more restricted context of dealing with negative or
hostile statements. A negative statement from an employee, for example, can quickly throw the appraisal
interview off course if it is responded to in kind.

E: I don't know how you can expect a person in my
position to do any better when I have to work under these antediluvian policies.

S: You can't blame the policies for your own failings.

The response may be true and right on target, but it
will arouse the defenses of the subordinate rather than
direct the interview to getting the job done. How much
better is this restatement of the feelings expressed:

E: I don't know how you can expect a person in my position to do any better when I have to work under these antediluvian policies.

S: You don't feel you should be held responsible for the results of outmoded policies.

Some people have a natural antipathy to making such a response. The more authoritarian you are, the more you will dislike responding in this way. There is an almost overwhelming tendency to think, "This guy is offering an excuse for his own poor performance and I'm not going to let him get away with it." A preachment like "You can't blame the policies for your own failings" is a natural product of this kind of attitude and is almost guaranteed to turn an interview into an argument.

"Well, do you expect me to agree with a puny excuse like that?" the authoritarian boss asks. No, we don't expect you to agree with it at all. Just *reflect back* to the speaker the feeling he expressed, and that will be the end of it. If you challenge it, fight it, decry it, deny it, or call it names, it will hang around and take the interview on a quick detour to disaster.

Restatement will not make a strong boss into a pansy, escalate permissiveness, or corrupt the boss with thoughts of disloyalty and treason. It will simply reflect the stated feelings of the speaker back to him, completely defusing them and heading off any foolish controversy that would endanger the objectives of the interview.

Subordinates whose performance is unsatisfactory but correctable will probably start out the interview unwilling to accept responsibility. They may try to shift the blame and defend themselves. If you continue to reflect their stated feelings back to them, they will gradually lose the urge to defend themselves and begin to accept responsibility. This is a growth process that you cannot argue them into. Your function is to provide an environment in which the employee can abandon his defenses and deal with his own inadequacies of performance.

AVOIDING DEFENSIVENESS IN YOURSELF

The tools of reducing defensiveness in your subordinate will work equally well to keep your own defenses down. In the course of some appraisal interviews you can expect to hear various complaints, criticisms, and attacks on the management as subordinates attempt to transfer the blame for their problems. Some of the complaints will be accurate, some preposterous.

Of this you can be sure: If you rise to defend against such comments, you will endanger the direction of the interview. Any time or effort spent debating the wisdom of policies, the weaknesses in your own leadership, or other matters only tangentially related to your subordinate's performance are wasted and diversionary.

This does not mean that you have to sit back and take all sorts of abuse. Very little of the employee's criticism will become abusive if you simply reflect it back. Even a subordinate who would like to start an argument to avoid talking about his performance will find it tough going if you use restatement to reflect his negative, argumentative feelings.

Silence, reassurance, and restatement are the tools of choice if you find yourself, your boss, the organization's policy, or anything else under attack. They will enable you to keep your cool and direct the interview to a constructive conclusion. And you don't have to wait until your next appraisal interview to give them a try. You can use them today.

CAREFUL WORDING

Unthinking, you stand blocking a doorway. A man comes along and says, "Get out of the way, stupid."

Or he says, "Excuse me, would you mind standing over here?" In either case, he gets you to move. The first approach gets your dander up and may lead to a hassle. Of the second approach we say, "The man has tact."

No one would say that a tactless person can't get things done. A football player doesn't tackle with tact. A hockey defenseman doesn't check a skater into the boards with tact. But in human relations, the person with tact is able to get things done without leaving a residue of hostility.

Skillful appraisal interviewing requires more than a passing interest in avoiding conflict, because we realize that it may destroy any hope of accomplishing our purposes. To the extent that being tactful will help avoid conflict, we need to be tactful. But what does it mean to be tactful? Let's look at some verbal devices that come under the general heading of tact.

Introductory phrases can soften questions that may otherwise sound blunt and more appropriate to cross-examination than to appraisal interviewing. For example, "Why did that happen?" can be softened by adding an introductory phrase: "Why do you think that happened?" The content of the question is the same, but the bluntness is reduced. Similarly, "Are you a good listener?" can be softened to "Would you say that you are a good listener?"

A whole array of introductory phrases can be used to make your questions less blunt:

"How did you happen to . . ."

"Why would you say that . . ."

"What caused it to . . ."

"What do you think about . . ."

"Do you feel that . . ."

"What has prompted you to . . ."

"How would you recommend that . . ."

Using the Right Word

There are some negative words often used in appraisal interviews that, however accurate, are not appropriate. They include such words as failure, weakness, inadequacy, shortcoming, and deficiency.

Using words like these to point to negative behavior that calls for correction is more likely to get defensiveness than correction. To avoid such negative words, we need to think positively about where we're trying to go rather than negatively about where we are now. Instantly, appropriate words begin coming to mind as we think ahead: growth, improvement, development, progress, success, achievement, accomplishment. The no-no words, for the most part, arise out of a negative orientation. An appraisal interview is held not to lament the past, but to plan for the future.

Avoiding Absolutes

Some of the most irritating remarks contain absolutes. When we say something like "You *always* handle that wrong," we mean not ever, even once, do you handle that right. If the victim of this condemnation can think of even one occasion when he did it right, he can prove the statement false. Absolutes admit no exceptions, and we would do well to leave out of our own speeches such gems as never, ever, always, every time, without exception, and invariably.

All of us would like to be given the benefit of the doubt that once in a while we do something right. Absolutes are the ultimate put-down and have no place in appraisal interviews.

Avoiding Profanity

In his attempt to avoid irritating extremes, the appraisal interviewer will do well to leave out profanity.

He may be able to confine it to nonthreatening statements, but there is always the risk that one of his
choice epithets will be directed against the subordinate, with predictable results.

Of profanity we know these things. To some people
it is offensive in any context, and offense is to be
avoided. To others profanity is appropriate only in
anger, and using it has the same effect as shouting,
accentuating the anger. Since there are few if any benefits of using profanity in appraisal interviews, the best
advice is to avoid it.

The simple technique of using the right words and
avoiding the wrong ones will keep the appraisal interview from being derailed. In the next chapter, we will
deal with practical methods for controlling the interview so that it meets the objectives set out for it.

16

CONTROLLING THE INTERVIEW

An appraisal interview can be a pleasant chat, but it must accomplish more than that. It is the supervisor's responsibility to control the interview so that it stays on the track and achieves its objective. This control should be subtle, not domineering, and is clearly essential to a productive interview.

The most difficult type of interview is the one aimed at the subordinate whose performance is not satisfactory but can be corrected. The objective is to get the subordinate's commitment to a plan to improve. Let's see how the supervisor can control the interview to achieve such an objective.

REACHING OBJECTIVES

The planning done before the interview pays off while the interview is in progress. You are in a position not just of getting through the interview, but of leading it toward the goal you have in mind.

Leading the employee to want to improve is the first task of the interview. This deceptively simple goal is achieved by judicious use of the skills described earlier. There is frank and open discussion about the job and some of your expectations. This discussion leads to recognition on the part of the employee that there is a gap between expectation and performance. It is essential that he *say that* and believe that. The boss's diagnosis is not likely to lead the employee to accept the problem readily.

Sometimes an appraisal interview deals with problems which the subordinate already recognized before the interview. He may not have spoken of them or done anything about them, but he knew they existed. The appraisal interview in this case serves not to enlighten him, but to bring him to the point of talking about the problems and planning to do something about them. Sometimes the subordinate is truly unaware of any gap between his performance and his boss's expectations. This is likely to be true when the boss has been negligent in telling his real expectations for the job or when there is little feedback to the employee between appraisals. When a subordinate learns for the first time that his performance is below expectations, there is some element of surprise, possibly mixed with other emotions. But the process is the same in either case: The subordinate and the supervisor have to work on solutions.

Once the employee has accepted the problem, it is relatively easy to lead him to want to improve. In fact, if the employee resists improvement, it is almost certain that he is really resisting the problem, or at least his role in the problem. When an employee wants to improve, his insights (unstated) usually progress in this order:

1. "I see there is a gap between your expectation and my performance."
2. "I see I have a part in that gap."
3. "I want to change the situation by eliminating whatever I contribute to the problem."

Communication would be improved if people actually spoke such thoughts directly, but very few do. Accordingly, the supervisor must watch for subtle signs that the employee sees (or doesn't see) the problem, accepts his part, and wants to improve. By using restatement and reassurance, the interviewer conditions himself to listen, and when he listens he hears these subtle cues.

Discussing possible ways to improve is the natural next step when the employee accepts a problem, acknowledges his part in it, and shows that he wants to improve. It may seem a simple step, but many people can readily accept a need to change and not have any idea how to begin. This is particularly true when the performance deficiency is the result of what may be termed a "character defect." What simple and obvious steps are to be taken by the employee who is habitually late, drinks too much, has careless work habits, berates subordinates, or fails to carry his share of the burden? Both supervisor and subordinate are in the area of soul and psyche with such needs, and the steps to be taken are seldom obvious.

It is easy for the boss confronting a problem such as alcoholism to revert to his authoritarian role and tell the employee, "Shape up or ship out." Indeed, this has been known to work. But, more realistically, there is a great struggle ahead for the employee and possibly for the medical profession, Alcoholics Anonymous, the company psychologist, and others.

Can the employee make the improvement he genuinely wants to make on his own? If he needs help, what kind of help should he get? What kind of support does he need on the job? At home?

Deciding on a plan and writing it down is the final step in bringing the interview to a productive conclusion. The plan is written down to remind the participants of what they agreed to; it is a private record. What should be written?

1. The nature of the improvement sought.
2. The quantity, if possible, of improvement sought.

3. One or more dates when progress is to be checked.
4. Who is going to do what.

When such a record is made, the interview will be more than a nice chat or a perfunctory ritual to please the personnel department. The ultimate result, of course, is yet to come. The interview doesn't make the changes, but it prepares the way by gaining the employee's acceptance and helping him develop a plan.

STAYING ON COURSE

The interviewing pattern just described provides a track for the appraisal interview to run. There is still the potential, of course, for unproductive interviews, not because they lack direction but because they can be allowed to stray off course. Here we will suggest some simple devices for holding straying to a minimum.

Stating the subject under discussion is the job of the supervisor. The employee has no way of knowing the subject unless he is told, as in this example:

S: This time of year I like to get together with each of you and discuss your performance. I've been reviewing your performance over the last year and there are several areas I'd like to talk over. The first is. . . .

This kind of introduction makes clear what is to be discussed and why. There is no reason to maintain any mystery about it; state the subject and begin.

Summarizing and changing the subject is another simple control device used to keep the interview on the track. It signals the end of one discussion and the beginning of another:

S: Well, we've talked about your interest in learning more about inventory valuation, and I've agreed to get you involved in that process next time around.

Now here's another area I'd like to talk to you about today.

Such statements keep the subordinate reminded of what you're doing and what progress you're making. Even with these very specific introductions, the subordinate may wander. If you find this happening, you'll have to pull the discussion back on the track.

Straying from the subject may come about just because the interview becomes too much of a conversation. Or the subordinate may raise some subject—such as salary—that doesn't fit the interview. Or the subordinate may bring up extraneous subjects in the hope of not having to talk about appropriate ones. You will have to recognize when the interview is going astray and pull it back on course.

Summarizing at the close goes naturally with writing up a brief summary of what has been agreed on, and serves to advise the employee that the interview has accomplished its goals and is now ending.

S: We've made good progress here today, Janet, and I hope you feel good about it too. I'll make some notes on the things we've agreed on and give you a copy.

STRIKING THE RIGHT BALANCE

The appraisal interview is a conversation that gets somewhere. It is formal in that it has objectives, runs on an orderly track, and results in concrete agreements. It is informal in that it is conversational, the subordinate does most of the talking, and the atmosphere is (ideally) relaxed.

Some supervisors have trouble striking a balance between the formal and the informal. They may be too stiff or too relaxed, too businesslike or too casual. It takes time to strike the right balance, but it's worth striving for.

Whether or not an appraisal interview brings about important changes is almost entirely up to the supervisor. It is he who does the appraisal, classifies the overall performance of the subordinate, selects the objectives and strategy, and leads the interview. If he does his job well, the subordinate does most of the talking, comes to new insights, and accepts responsibility for his performance.

17

QUESTIONS AND ANSWERS ABOUT APPRAISAL INTERVIEWING

IN WHAT SETTING SHOULD THE APPRAISAL INTERVIEW BE HELD?

Very briefly, it should be private and isolated against interruptions. "Private" means that others cannot hear the interview through the walls or door and cannot come in and out of the room for various purposes. "Isolated" means that neither the telephone nor any person will interrupt the meeting except in a true emergency.

It may be necessary to leave the normal work premises to conduct the interview. The supervisor should do everything in his power to obtain private quarters and to eliminate possible interruptions. There is little hope for an interview that can be overheard by others or that is constantly interrupted by matters that appear to be of greater importance than the subordinate and his performance.

HOW WELL CAN THE APPRAISAL INTERVIEW WORK WHEN THE BOSS AND SUBORDINATE REALLY DON'T COMMUNICATE?

It must be very clear that it cannot work at all. In such a situation the supervisor should work on the interpersonal skills described in this book and attempt to smooth the relationship first. The probability is very low that the interview will be successful while animosity or misunderstanding reigns.

SOME FEEDBACK ABOUT PERFORMANCE SHOULD NOT BE LEFT UNTIL THE NEXT APPRAISAL. WHICH KINDS?

In general, two kinds of feedback should be given in day-to-day supervision and not left until the next appraisal. One is information about critical matters that affect safety, production, other employees, and the subordinate's own job security. The other includes discussion of minor annoyances (like not turning off the lights when leaving) that are simply inappropriate in the appraisal interview.

Certainly anything that threatens a person's job, interferes with the rights or work of others, or creates safety hazards is too urgent to leave unresolved until the next appraisal. Such matters must be taken up in routine supervision as they occur. Likewise, to keep the appraisal interview from being cluttered with minor details, trivia must be handled in day-to-day contacts with the subordinate.

HOW MUCH DISCUSSION OF THE EMPLOYEE'S SALARY SHOULD BE INCLUDED IN AN APPRAISAL INTERVIEW?

None. The supervisor should not bring it up. If the employee brings it up and insists on discussing it, set a date to do that. An appraisal interview in which salary is a significant part will not deal effectively with matters of performance.

HOW CAN THE SUPERVISOR GET THE SUBORDINATE TO DO MOST OF THE TALKING AND STILL CONTROL THE INTERVIEW?

He has two ways to control an appraisal interview. One is to do all the talking, diagnose the problems, prescribe the solutions, and impose his will on the subordinate. This is guaranteed to keep the interview under control but will produce no lasting benefits.

The other way is to control by stating the subject areas, asking questions related to it, drawing the subordinate out, leading him subtly, and summarizing. The subordinate will still do most of the talking, but the supervisor will control by advance preparation and the use of learned skills. "Control" means management of a process, not domination of people.

CAN YOU SAY ONE GOOD WORD FOR PRINTED APPRAISAL FORMS?

Yes.

ISN'T IT ESSENTIAL TO KEEP A RECORD OF PERFORMANCE APPRAISALS ON AN EMPLOYEE?

Essential to whom and for what? The error-strewn process of growing, learning, and maturing is the private and personal adventure of each employee. Even if it were possible to record absolutely objective, quantitative appraisals of an employee, of what possible use could they be to anyone other than the immediate supervisor? The record of judgments can be used in many ways to hurt the employee, but the ways it could be used to help him or the company are obscure.

The immediate supervisor may want to keep a copy of the most recent appraisal on each employee so that he can review commitments and progress. The employee should have a copy for the same purposes. But whether a continuing record of performance appraisals is essential to anyone is a good question. The answer is probably no.

WHAT IS THE PYGMALION SYNDROME?

The thesis of G. B. Shaw's *Pygmalion* is that progress in British society is determined not by ability or perseverance, but by excellence in speaking the language. Extended, the Pygmalion theme is that of the self-fulfilling prophecy. Johnny is said to be stupid, unable to learn, and true to the prophecy he fails in school. (If he had been said to be smart, he would have succeeded.)

In business, industry, and government, the recorded judgments of supervisors can be used to "predict" an employee's future. His supervisor sees him as "tactless" or "ambitious," and these appellations are used to *determine* his future. The employee's future is determined not by what he can do or become, but by what a few others have said about him.

Of this we are sure: If there were no files of appraisals, the Pygmalion syndrome would virtually disappear.

ISN'T IT TRUE THAT MOST IMPROVEMENTS MADE BY SUBORDINATES ARE IN JOB PERFORMANCE RATHER THAN IN OVERCOMING "CHARACTER DEFECTS"?

It is certainly true that it is *easier* to get improvements in performance than to effect changes in a person's characteristics and habits. It is easier, for example, to teach a worker to use his machine properly than to overcome chronic lateness or alcohol dependency. But this does not mean that there is no hope for character improvements.

What can be done is limited primarily by the supervisor and his view of people. If he sees people as stubborn, unyielding, incapable of change, his subordinates will probably prove to be that way. If he sees potential in every person and accepts that change can and does happen, sometimes miraculously, his subordinates will probably reflect that.

Studies indicate that more than 90 percent of those who lose their jobs lose them for some "character defect" rather than because they are unable to do the work. The great potential for change and growth, then, lies in what people are, not in what they can do. A supervisor who recognizes the reality of human potential can be an agent of change.

I HAVE A SUBORDINATE WHO SEEMS TO HAVE VERY LITTLE IDEA OF WHAT IS EXPECTED OF HIM. HOW SHOULD I HANDLE HIS APPRAISAL INTERVIEW?

You can hardly appraise a subordinate fairly against standards of which he knows little or nothing. Spend the time you would normally spend in the appraisal and the interview informing him of what your expectations are, and making sure he understands them. Let him know that there will be an appraisal later on (perhaps in 60 or 90 days) and that his performance will be measured against these expectations. Be sure he understands that you are at fault for failing to make the job expectations clear to him.

IF GOOD PERFORMANCE CANNOT BE TAKEN AS ASSURANCE OF PROMOTION, WHAT CAN?

Even in the best-managed organizations it is impossible to predict future personnel needs and promotion patterns with any accuracy. Openings occur and the people presumed to be the best qualified are selected to fill them. In the best-managed organizations, good past performance is the major criterion for such selections. Even so, other well-qualified people are passed over with each filling of a vacancy just because there is only one vacancy and only one person who can fill it. It is said, for example, that some colleges turn down as many well-qualified applicants as they accept. This practice reflects the capacity of the institutions to absorb and not the qualifications of many who apply.

Employees should be taught that it is unreasonable to expect prompt promotion whenever their performance is judged satisfactory. Each must develop the patience to watch (1) what happens to himself in the system, (2) what happens to competent people in the system, and (3) what happens to incompetent people. If the employee sees that the competent are rewarded with promotion, he may assume that his continued competence will *in time* be rewarded also. If, on the other hand, the employee perceives that the system rewards incompetence and fails to reward competence, he has two choices. He can adopt the form and level of incompetence that he thinks will win him a promotion, or he can begin looking for an organization where his competence will more likely be rewarded.

On a short-term basis, there is not necessarily a direct correlation between good performance and promotion. In a well-managed organization, such a correlation exists in the long term.

IS THERE REALLY A GREAT DANGER THAT AN APPRAISAL INTERVIEW WILL END UP IN AN ARGUMENT?

There definitely is. A far greater danger, however, is that the supervisor will dominate the interview and that the employee will submit and never express his real feelings and goals. The insensitive supervisor sees such an encounter as successful because he "won" it, not realizing that he gained nothing.

Such an interview may actually be worse than one in which an argument occurs. At least the latter exposes the disagreement and hostility so that both parties can see it. If these are recognized and jointly resolved, great progress has been made.

Supervisors recognize that they can prevent argument by dominating the interview. This usually destroys the purpose of the interview. The objective of avoiding argument should not be allowed to override methodology. Skillful interviewing will also avoid argument, but it will leave open the possibility of achieving the desired results.

TO WHAT EXTENT SHOULD THE SUPERVISOR "TAKE OVER" HIS SUBORDINATE'S NEEDS OR PROBLEMS?

Ownership of the subordinate's problems must not be shifted at any time. The subordinate has the problems and is responsible for solving them. The supervisor or employer's role is limited to helping the employee recognize the problems, make a plan, and carry it through. The employer can help the employee with his problems in a number of ways, but the responsibility must rest with the employee.

HAVEN'T YOU OVERSTATED THE NEED FOR APPRAISAL INTERVIEWING?

If anything, the need is understated. Supervisors typically think their subordinates know a lot more about their own performance than the subordinates in fact know. A vast proportion of employees at all levels know little or nothing of how well their performance matches expectations. Many more know part of the story, but precious few know everything they need to know about their own performance.

INDEX

119